MacAddict

Guide to

Making Music with
GARAGEBAND

Jay Shaffer

Gary Rosenzweig

800 East 96th Street
Indianapolis, Indiana 46240

MacAddict Guide to Making Music with GarageBand™

International Standard Book Number: 0-7897-3226-2

Library of Congress Catalog Card Number: 2004104258

Printed in the United States of America

First Printing: June 2004

07   06   05   04   4   3   2   1

Trademarks

All terms mentioned in this book that are known to be trademarks or service marks have been appropriately capitalized. Que Publishing cannot attest to the accuracy of this information. Use of a term in this book should not be regarded as affecting the validity of any trademark or service mark.

GarageBand is a trademark of Apple Computer, Inc.

Warning and Disclaimer

Every effort has been made to make this book as complete and as accurate as possible, but no warranty or fitness is implied. The information provided is on an "as is" basis. The authors and the publisher shall have neither liability nor responsibility to any person or entity with respect to any loss or damages arising from the information contained in this book.

Bulk Sales

Que Publishing offers excellent discounts on this book when ordered in quantity for bulk purchases or special sales. For more information, please contact

U.S. Corporate and Government Sales
1-800-382-3419
corpsales@pearsontechgroup.com

For sales outside of the U.S., please contact

International Sales
1-317-428-3341
international@pearsontechgroup.com

Que Publishing   QUE®

Publisher
Paul Boger

Associate Publisher
Greg Wiegand

Executive Editor
Rick Kughen

Development Editor
Laura Norman

Managing Editor
Charlotte Clapp

Project Editor
Tonya Simpson

Production Editor
Megan Wade

Indexer
Ken Johnson

Proofreader
Wendy Ott

Publishing Coordinator
Sharry Gregory

Interior Designer
Anne Jones

Page Layout
Stacey Richwine-DeRome

MacAddict

Publisher
Chris Coelho

Editor In Chief
Rik Myslewski

Technical Editor
Kris Fong

Cover Designer
Mark Rosenthal

Future Network USA

Editorial Director
Jon Phillips

AT A GLANCE

CONTENTS

3 Recording Your Own Music with Software Instruments   31

G MIDI Implementation Chart   221

H General MIDI Drum Key Map   223

I Online Resources   225

Index   229

About the Authors

Jay Shaffer is a freelance sound designer, audio engineering consultant, and music composer. He has over 20 years' experience in the recording industry and has produced and recorded several award-winning albums as well as having composed music for computer games, videos, and films.

Although he cut his teeth on Commodore 64s and Amigas, Jay is a certified Mac addict and is now on his eighth Macintosh since 1986. He also administers the Mac Audio Guy Web site, a resource for Mac audio professionals and enthusiasts.

Jay, a Colorado native, lives in Golden, Colorado, with his wife Annie and his dogs, Iggy Pup and Greta Garbone. In his spare time Jay enjoys spoiling his grandchildren and racing sports cars.

This is Jay's first book.

Professional home page: http://macaudioguy.com

Personal home page: http://jayshaffer.com/

Email: mag@jayshaffer.com

Gary Rosenzweig is the chief engineer, founder, and owner of CleverMedia, a game and multimedia development company in Denver, Colorado. He has written 10 books on Macromedia Director and Flash.

Gary has degrees from both Drexel University in Philadelphia and the University of North Carolina in Chapel Hill. He has been building multimedia projects since 1989. CleverMedia was founded in 1995 and has produced more than 250 Shockwave and Flash games for CleverMedia's sites and other companies.

Gary lives in Denver, Colorado, with his wife Debby, daughter Luna, cat Lucy, and dog Natasha. Debby owns The Attic Bookstore (http://atticbookstore.com/), a used bookstore in Denver. Besides computers and the Internet, Gary also enjoys film, camping, classic science fiction books, writing, and video games.

Some of Gary's other Que Publishing books are *Special Edition Using Director MX*, *Advanced Lingo for Games*, and *Flash MX ActionScript for Fun and Games*.

Personal home page: http://garyrosenzweig.com/

Email: http://garyrosenzweig.com/email.html

Dedication

Jay Shaffer
*For my patient wife, Annie, my lovely stepdaughter, Ursula,
and my precious grandchildren, Kyra and Jared.*

Gary Rosenzweig
*For my daughter, Luna, who is still young enough to
think that her dad is a good piano player.*

Acknowledgments

Jay Shaffer

Thanks to my coauthor, teacher, friend, and former employer, Gary Rosenzweig.

Bil Taylor for singing and playing on the demo tunes.

My parents—I'm totally sorry about the 1970s.

My brothers and sister: Jeff, Scott, and Karla.

The Little Sisters of No Mercy and Clan Kennedy.

The Ingenius alumni.

Steve Jobs for Macs and GarageBand.

The Fat Man, my unwitting mentor.

Brian Eno, for inspiration.

Gary Rosenzweig

Thanks to Jay Shaffer for letting me come along on this book project.

Very special thanks go to William Follett and to all the people I have had the pleasure of working with in the past.

Thanks to my family for their continuing lifetime of support: Jacqueline, Jerry, and Larry Rosenzweig; Rebecca Jacob; and Barbara and Richard Shifrin.

The most thanks go to my wife, Debby, for her never-ending love and support.

Thanks to the artists that have inspired me to love music over the years: The Beatles, Juliana Hatfield, Frank Sinatra, Ludwig Van Beethoven, Madonna, Liz Phair, Muddy Waters, Pink Floyd, The Donnas, Duran Duran, B.B. King, Led Zeppelin, Cyndi Lauper, Johann Sebastian Bach, Maganpop, Rush, Bobby Darin, The Who, Taj Mahal, Cowboy Junkies, Creedence Clearwater Revival, John Williams, Eric Clapton, Courtney Love, James Brown, John Lee Hooker, Jethro Tull, Wolfgang Amadeus Mozart, Louis Armstrong, Joe Walsh, Tori Amos, and Neil Young.

From Both

To all the people at Que and *MacAddict* who helped put this book together: Acquisitions and Development Editor Laura Norman, Technical Editor Kris Fong (Senior Editor at *MacAddict*), Project Editor Tonya Simpson, Production Editor Megan Wade, Indexer Ken Johnson, Proofreader Wendy Ott, and Page Layout Technician Stacey Richwine-DeRome.

We Want to Hear from You!

As the reader of this book, *you* are our most important critic and commentator. We value your opinion and want to know what we're doing right, what we could do better, what areas you'd like to see us publish in, and any other words of wisdom you're willing to pass our way.

As an associate publisher for Que Publishing, I welcome your comments. You can email or write me directly to let me know what you did or didn't like about this book—as well as what we can do to make our books better.

Please note that I cannot help you with technical problems related to the topic of this book. We do have a User Services group, however, where I will forward specific technical questions related to the book.

When you write, please be sure to include this book's title and author as well as your name, email address, and phone number. I will carefully review your comments and share them with the author and editors who worked on the book.

Email: feedback@quepublishing.com

Mail: Greg Wiegand
           Associate Publisher
           Que Publishing
           800 East 96th Street
           Indianapolis, IN 46240 USA

For more information about this book or another Que Publishing title, visit our Web site at www.quepublishing.com. Type the ISBN (excluding hyphens) or the title of a book in the Search field to find the page you're looking for.

INTRODUCTION

When GarageBand was announced in January 2004, we immediately knew that it was something special. Musicians and Mac lovers rushed to the Apple stores when iLife '04 was released later that month to get their hands on it.

The exclamation, "This is the tool I have been waiting for!" was heard around the world that day. GarageBand was an instant software hit.

GarageBand is a revolutionary tool that lets you create songs using your own compositions and premade loops. You can plug your keyboard, guitar, or microphone into your Mac and use it as a recording studio. Then, you can export your songs for use in audio CDs, downloadable files, and video soundtracks.

We quickly saw the need for a book on GarageBand and began writing. This book is the result.

We've created something for beginners and experts alike. It covers the basics but is deep enough to teach new tricks to old dogs as well.

Whether you make a living from music or just enjoy music, GarageBand is a wonderful and fun tool. We think we have created a book that will help you find even more profit and enjoyment from it. We hope you enjoy this book as much as we enjoyed writing it.

WHO SHOULD READ THIS BOOK

This book is geared to just about anyone who wants to use GarageBand. Whether you are new to music, new to Macs, or an expert at both, you will find that this book is a useful guide.

MUSICIANS

With the introduction of GarageBand, Apple is telling musicians: "We want you!" Rather than relying on third-party software to make the Mac useful to you, Apple has taken it upon itself to practically build in music-making software by making GarageBand available as part of the $49 iLife '04 package.

This book guides you through the GarageBand interface and helps you take full advantage of what the software can do for you.

MAC USERS

Many Mac users start by buying their computers for one thing or the other: doing term papers, surfing the Internet, desktop publishing, and so on. But, they soon find that their Macs are more useful than they could have possibly imagined.

Now Mac users have yet another thing they can do with their Macs: make music. Even people who can't play any instrument at all can use GarageBand to put together loops and create songs.

This book shows you how to use GarageBand, and it does not assume that you are a virtuoso or that you can even play Chop Sticks.

PEOPLE NEW TO BOTH

With GarageBand, Apple is hoping to make converts. Many people find themselves switching to Macs as new software gets introduced. iPhoto brought over some people interested in digital photography, the iPod brought over some music lovers, and iMovie and iDVD brought over home video amateurs and beginning filmmakers.

With GarageBand, many musicians and music lovers will find themselves buying their first Mac. This book guides you through learning GarageBand even if you are not familiar with the Mac interface.

HOW THIS BOOK IS ORGANIZED

This book starts off with the simplest aspects of GarageBand. Chapter 1, "Getting Started with GarageBand," helps you get it installed; then Chapter 2, "Making Music with Apple Loops," shows you how to create a song without any musical background at all.

Chapters 3–5 show musicians how to record their own compositions using MIDI keyboards, instruments like guitars, and vocals through a microphone.

Even non-musicians may find that working with GarageBand is so easy it brings out talent they never thought they had.

Then Chapter 6, "Editing and Mixing Your Music," goes on to show you more advanced production techniques.

Musicians and non-musicians alike can then use Chapter 7, "Finishing Up," to learn how to export songs to iTunes, burn them to CDs, and send them to friends.

Chapters 8–10 deal with advanced techniques like making your own instruments and loops.

The appendixes include valuable reference material, such as information on how to expand GarageBand and set up your studio, lists of MIDI instruments, and a MIDI drum map. You can also find a list of online resources so you know where to get the latest GarageBand news and techniques.

BEYOND THE BOOK

This book includes many examples. You can re-create each example by following along with the tutorials. If you wish to compare your work with the files we generated while writing this book, you can visit the book's Web site:

http://macaudioguy.com/gbb/downloads/

We will also be posting updates here:

http://macaudioguy.com/gbb/support/

GETTING STARTED WITH GARAGEBAND

IN THIS CHAPTER:

➤ Learn what GarageBand is and what it will do for you

➤ Get a quick overview of the installation process

➤ Learn how to optimize your Mac for better GarageBand performance

For many amateur musicians, GarageBand is the tool we have been waiting for our whole lives. It is a recording studio inside your Mac, complete with session musicians.

Sure, there has been plenty of software before that allows us to express ourselves musically through our computers. But these expensive applications are for professionals—experts. What about the rest of us? You don't have to know much about music or software or even own an instrument to use GarageBand.

So put down your copy of *Rolling Stone*, tune your guitar, and fire up your Mac. Let's get ready to rock and roll!

WHAT IS GARAGEBAND?

According to Apple CEO Steve Jobs, "GarageBand does for music creation what iMovie did for video and iPhoto did for photos—makes the creative process easy and affordable for everyone."

GarageBand combines functionality formerly only found in different pieces of software. It combines this functionality in such a way to make us wonder why it was ever done any other way.

But trying to understand GarageBand—to really see what it is capable of—is not easy. That is because you can do so many different things with it:

- **Select from prerecorded loops**—You can select from a library of hundreds of prerecorded loops to add to your song. You can build a song completely out of these loops, or just use them to compliment your own recordings.

- **Record audio**—With GarageBand you can plug a microphone or instrument, such as a guitar, directly into your Macintosh and record while you sing or play.

- **Edit audio**—Once you have a recorded audio track, you can trim it, cut it apart, and even duplicate or loop parts of the recording.

- **Apply effects to audio**—You can take your recorded audio track and apply effects to make it sound unique.

- **Record MIDI instruments**—If you have a keyboard or other digital instrument, you can record the notes you play and use them in GarageBand.

- **Edit MIDI recordings**—Once you have recorded your tunes, you can edit the notes. You can also cut the recording apart and duplicate or loop parts of it.

- **Modify MIDI recordings**—When you have digitally recorded tracks, you can change the instrument used to play the track and even change the tempo or key.

- **Create instruments**—You can use one of the many built-in digital instruments to play your recorded digital track, or you can create a custom sound by adjusting the properties of an existing GarageBand instrument's sound.

- **Mix recordings**—You can record multiple tracks with analog or digital equipment and then mix them together, layering them on top of each other.

- **Play and record at the same time**—You can listen to your song creation and record a new track at the same time, allowing you to play along with your song and add to it.

- **Export to iTunes and beyond**—You can take your GarageBand recordings and export them to iTunes. Then, with the help of iTunes and other software, you can convert them to MP3 and show off your creations to the rest of the world.

note

GarageBand comes with more than 1,000 prerecorded loops. You can add another 2,000 loops with the $99 GarageBand Jam Pack.

So, imagine you want to compose a song. Maybe you have been playing around with a simple melody on your keyboard. Now it is time to put something together that other people can listen to.

In Chapters 2–6 we'll look at how to use GarageBand in detail. But for now, let's just turn away from the computer screen and imagine.

You open GarageBand and start a new song. Using the Loop Browser, you audition several drum loops until you find a drum loop that fits your style. You make that your first track and set it to play for 3 minutes.

Now you play that drum loop, and while it is playing, you play your keyboard, which is hooked up to your Mac. You fill in the melody over the drums. When you are done playing, you can play back the song and hear your melody repeated, along with the drum loop behind it.

Then you pick a nice bass line to compliment your melody. Perhaps a little ambient acoustic guitar as well, but only later in the song.

You go back in to your melody and start editing it on the computer screen. Some of your notes were off, but that is easily fixed. You take one part and have it repeat a few times before the next part. A tweak here and a tweak there.

Then you decide the piano is not the best instrument to represent your melody. So, you change it to a pop organ. You also adjust the bass line to a louder slap bass.

Next, you plug your guitar in to the computer and play the song again. When it gets to the right part, you play a funky guitar solo and it is recorded into yet another track. Play it back again and adjust the volume on the solo so it fits in just right.

To finish it off, you invite your attractive neighbor over. You know, the one that sings in the church choir, but you know that they are really dying to be a pop star. You plug in a microphone and you do a duet with the deep, meaningful lyrics you just wrote.

Then you export the song out to iTunes. You put a copy on your iPod and burn a CD for your neighbor.

Later that night you upload it to the Internet. The next day, you get a call from a major label and three months later you are a huge star.

Okay. Technically, we will not be covering the last little bit there in this book. But, you can figure that out for yourself.

As you can see, GarageBand can be a lot of fun. It gives the amateur musician most of the recording and production power of a big studio, but without the price and steep learning curve.

Let's install GarageBand and then give it a try.

> **note**
>
> GarageBand comes with more than 50 virtual instruments. You can tweak settings to make your own or get more than 100 additional instrument sounds with GarageBand Jam Pack.

INSTALLING GARAGEBAND

If you purchased the iLife '04 package, which includes GarageBand, you received both an installer CD and an installer DVD. Both iDVD and GarageBand are only available on the install DVD, so obviously you will need a Mac with a DVD-ROM drive to install GarageBand.

In addition to a DVD drive, you will need a pretty recent Mac as well. According to Apple, the system requirements are a G3 600MHz or faster, 256MB of memory, a 1024 × 768 display, Mac OS 10.2.8, QuickTime 6.4, and 4.3GB of disk space.

To begin the installation, insert the iLife '04 Install DVD and follow these steps:

1. When the Install DVD window appears, double-click the install icon. Be forewarned that the entire iLife '04 installation will take up a whopping 4.6GB of hard disk space.

2. The next step is to provide your administrator password. If you are running Mac OS X 10.3 Panther, the installer will scan your computer to determine which programs it can install; then you will be asked for your administrator password. If you are running Mac OS X 10.2 Jaguar, which is the minimum system requirement for iLife '04, you will just be asked for your administrator password.

3. After you read the software license agreement—you do read the software license agreement, don't you—you can click Agree to accept your fate.

4. The next dialog will ask you where you would like to install iLife '04 if you have multiple hard drives; if you only have one hard drive, you will be taken immediately to the all-important Installation Type dialog in the installer. This dialog should look like Figure 1.1.

FIGURE 1.1
The installation dialog isn't that exciting, but you can't avoid it.

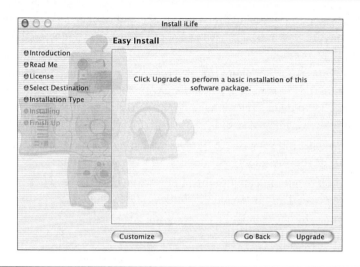

5 It is at this juncture that you must decide whether you want to install the entire iLife '04 package, which includes iPhoto 4, iTunes 4.2, iMovie 4, iDVD 4, and finally GarageBand 1.0. You could also perform a custom installation. Clicking the Customize button allows you to choose which parts of the iLife package you would like to install.

If you have limited hard disk space available, you might want to choose to install only GarageBand. Be aware that GarageBand alone will require 2.5GB of free hard disk space. To install GarageBand only, you need to uncheck the packages that you do not wish to install. Figure 1.2 shows GarageBand only checked to install.

FIGURE 1.2
Checking only GarageBand helps you save gigabytes from those nasty freeloaders that hog up your hard drive!

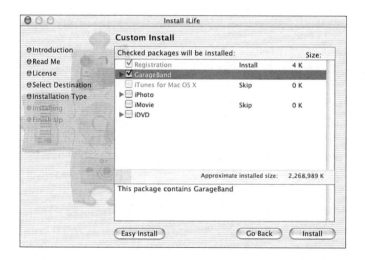

After deciding upon an installation option and clicking Install you will be presented with a registration dialog where you can decide if you wish to register your software at this time. After making a selection in this dialog, the installation process will begin and eventually you will be rewarded with a dialog which informs you that your software was indeed successfully installed, as shown in Figure 1.3. Click the close button to terminate the installation process.

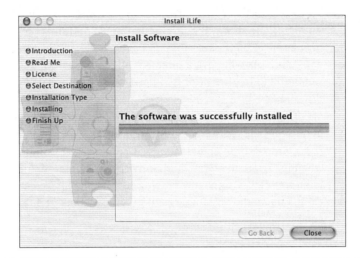

FIGURE 1.3
Installation success!
Failure is not an option.

Now that GarageBand is installed, let's build our first song. Then we'll continue to build our knowledge of how GarageBand incorporates different elements to make even more complex songs. Later, in Chapter 8, "Making Your Own Software and Real Instruments," we'll look at your computer set-up and see how you can adjust your hardware and software to get better performance out of GarageBand.

WHAT TO EXPECT FROM GARAGEBAND ON YOUR MAC

Turning a computer into a musical instrument and recording studio is very processor intensive. While most people tend not to read the system requirements too closely, with GarageBand, you need to take the system requirements very seriously.

If you have a G3-powered Mac you can only expect four or five Real Instrument tracks before running into the dreaded `Unable to Continue` error message. While this may serve as a viable alternative to the horribly noisy cassette 4-track port-a-studios that many garage bands still use, it is hardly a 32-track super studio that many users expect.

In fact, I first launched GarageBand on a 450MHz G4 with 800MB of RAM and was shocked to run into an `Unable to continue` error after only 5 tracks of using loops and Software Instruments. After upgrading to a 1.25GHz processor, I was able to run 10–15 tracks.

note

If you have a G3 Mac and are running OS 10.3 Panther, you may be presented with an installation dialog asking if you wish to install software instruments with GarageBand. Be aware that software instruments are extremely processor intensive and may not work properly on a G3 Mac. Even without software instruments, you will still be able to record audio and utilize Real Instrument loops and other functions with GarageBand.

So, how many tracks can you expect to get from your Mac? The answer depends on several factors. First is processor speed. Apple's published system requirements state a minimum 600MHz G3 to run GarageBand. You can get GarageBand to barely run on a 256MHz G3, but to get 32 tracks out of GarageBand, you will probably need a G5 dual 2GHz.

Secondly, the more RAM the better. 512MB seems to be about the minimum that will work, whereas 1GB might be sufficient. With RAM prices being low, RAM expansion is your best "bang for the buck" in improving GarageBand's performance.

Another thing that will help GarageBand's performance is making sure that it is the only application that is running. Background applications like your email program and AppleTalk will have a negative effect on performance. You can also set GarageBand to have priority on processor usage (see the next section, "Setting Priorities").

Finally, it is important to manage your use of both effects and Software Instruments in GarageBand. With plain old audio tracks with no effects or audio loop tracks, the Mac's processor is only dealing with playing back multiple audio streams. However, when using audio effects and Software Instruments, the processor is taxed with intensive digital signal processing (DSP) calculations and, along with its usual critical timing, audio streaming, and graphical tasks, it doesn't take long before it simply can't keep up.

SETTING PRIORITIES

If you are comfortable in dealing with OS X's Unix guts, you can adjust the priority that your Mac's processor gives to GarageBand. If you are a Mac power user, here are some things you can do to improve performance. If you are not an expert, however, feel free to skip this part and come back to it later if you find you are having problems with the system getting bogged down.

After launching GarageBand, go to your Applications ⋯⟩ Utilities folder and you will find a program called either Process Viewer (OS X 10.2.x), see Figure 1.4, or Activity Monitor (OS X 10.3.x.), see Figure 1.5. This nifty little program allows you to see just how much of your system is being hogged by GarageBand. There are two important pieces of information that the Process Viewer/Activity Monitor provides. First, it shows approximately how much of your CPU is being used by GarageBand, and second, it shows GarageBand's process ID number.

Jot down the process ID number (PID) for GarageBand, as you will need that number for the next step in the process. Next, go to the Applications ⋯⟩ Utilities folder and launch the Terminal Application. At the command prompt type in the following command (where *PID* is the process number of GarageBand that you jotted down) and then press Return:

```
sudo renice -19 PID
```

FIGURE 1.4
The Process viewer (OS X 10.2.x) is a window into the shenanigans inside your Mac.

FIGURE 1.5
The Activity Monitor (OS X 10.3.x) is sort of like Big Brother for your Mac.

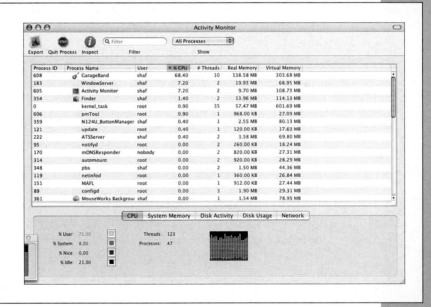

The result should look something like Figure 1.6. You can close the Terminal application at this point and start using GarageBand, taking comfort in the thought that you've set GarageBand to a high priority—even though you may not have the faintest idea of what that means.

FIGURE 1.6
This is the Terminal showing the renice command. Unfortunately, there is no "be nice" command.

Don't want to mess with all that Unix weenie stuff? How about a piece of freeware that makes it easier? Aim your browser to http://www.lachoseinteractive.net/en/products/processwizard/. Launch the ProcessWizard and you can set the priority of any process from your Desktop menu bar, as shown in Figure 1.7.

FIGURE 1.7
The ProcessWizard menu is much nicer than Terminal, unless you're into that sort of thing.

After launching GarageBand, pull down ProcessWizard from the menu bar and move the priority slider for GarageBand all the way to the right. Violà!

MAKING MUSIC WITH APPLE LOOPS

2

Ready to make some music? That usually means years of musical training, teaming up with a band, and tons of practice. Not to mention the van you'll need to carry the drums and amplifiers around.

Nah, forget that. That's so...twentieth century. Instead, just click the GarageBand icon in your Mac OS X dock. Wasn't that easier?

Now you are a just a few clicks and drags away from making your first song.

STARTING A NEW SONG

If this is the first time you have used GarageBand, the New Project dialog will appear. Otherwise, you can bring up the New Project dialog by selecting File ⋯▹ New. Figure 2.1 shows the New Project dialog.

To begin, you can use the default filename My Song or type your own song title in the Save As field. You can save your project in the default GarageBand folder or choose a different one by clicking the inverted triangle button to the right of the Save As field and navigating and selecting your desired folder.

FIGURE 2.1
The New Project dialog is your first step to super-stardom.

SETTING THE TEMPO AND KEY

The other settings in the New Project dialog let you set some basic information about your song: the tempo, time signature, and musical key.

The tempo of a song determines the speed at which the notes are played. This is measured in beats per minute, or bpm as shown in Figure 2.1. However, for some reason the number is shown to the right of the Time pop-up menu, even though it relates more to the tempo above it.

The *time signature*, or *time*, of your song determines how notes in your song relate to the tempo. It consists of two numbers. The first is the number of beats in each measure. The second determines the duration of a note that equals one beat.

The *key* of your song is a setting for more experienced composers. It helps GarageBand to find loops that match the rest of your composition. Beats? Measures? Key? Don't panic and call your old guitar teacher yet. You'll find that the default settings for time and key are good enough for general-purpose music creation, so leave them as-is for now.

CLEARING THE TRACK WINDOW

After you click the Create button, the My Song project is created and the main GarageBand window opens. Figure 2.2 shows the main GarageBand window. It will be your starting point for every new composition.

GarageBand conveniently puts an empty Grand Piano track in the window for you. Convenient, that is, if you plan to start playing the piano right away. But not so convenient if you plan to start adding some Apple Loops like we will do in this chapter.

A *track* is single slice of music that makes up one layer of sound in your song. For instance, you can have a drum track, a bass track, a guitar track, a vocal track, and so on. You can have multiple tracks of the same type—there is no limit. For instance, a simple song may only have 4 tracks, while a symphonic piece may have 40.

tip

All GarageBand song files are saved with the extension .band. The default location for these files is in your Music folder in a new folder named GarageBand.

note

Later you will learn that you can select the Master track and select Track ┄┄> Show Track Info to change the tempo, time signature, and key of the song after you've started composing.

FIGURE 2.2
The GarageBand window is lighter and less expensive than a recording studio.

Loop Browser Button

Since we'll be using only premade Apple Loops in this chapter, we'll want to delete this empty Grand Piano track. To do this, follow these steps:

1. First make sure the track is selected. Click the icon of the piano keyboard or the label Grand Piano.

2. Select Track ⋯⟩ Delete Track (or just press ⌘-Delete).

Now you will have a completely empty song. We can change that once you learn how to use the Loop Browser.

USING THE LOOP BROWSER

To open the Loop Browser, click the third button from the left at the bottom of the GarageBand window. This button looks like an eye and was pointed out previously in Figure 2.2.

The Loop Browser takes many forms. The default look for the Loop Browser is how you see it in Figure 2.3. It shows a set of 30 buttons, an empty list to the right, and some extra controls at the bottom.

So what you see is a series of buttons with names like Urban, Relaxed, and Ensemble. These buttons allow you to define what type of loop you are looking for.

tip
You can always know which track is selected because information in the Tracks and Mixer columns is highlighted in green.

note
You might also see a small window with a keyboard in it. We'll use this window in Chapter 3, "Recording Your Own Music with Software Instruments." For now, you can close it.

FIGURE 2.3
The Loop Browser is like 1,000 musicians auditioning for you any time you want.

BROWSING LOOPS

tip

You can expand the Loop Browser to show 63 instead of 30 buttons. To do this, click and drag in the empty space in the large brushed metal control bar between the upper tracks portion of the window and the lower Loop Browser portion of the window.

Okay, so now imagine that you are a famous rock star. Your ego has grown so big that you just left your group to start a solo career. But you can't play all the instruments yourself. So now you are auditioning musicians for your new band.

The next room is full of musicians of every type—drummers, bass guitarists, triangle players, and so on. Now you get to call them in, one by one, and see what they sound like.

First, narrow down the musicians a bit. For instance, to try out drummers, click the Drums button in the Loop Browser. You'll notice two changes. First, several of the other buttons are now inactive. This is because they conflict with your selection so far. For instance, the Piano button is now inactive because you only want to hear Drums.

The second thing that changed is that the list on the right side of the Loop Browser is now populated with all the drum loops. There are a lot of them. So let's narrow it down a bit by clicking another button. Click the Country button. This narrows the selections down to only three. There are three loops that correspond to Drums and Country. Figure 2.4 shows the Loop Browser now.

FIGURE 2.4
After clicking Drums and Country, you've narrowed your loop choices down to three. All the others have gone packing.

By using the buttons, you are effectively performing a keyword search using predetermined keywords. For instance, the previous example was a search for "Drums, Country." Each loop has a set of keywords attached to it. The three loops that you get as a result of the previous example all have both "Drums" and "Country" as keywords.

SEARCHING LOOPS

You can also search loops by their names. This ignores the keywords attached to the loops and, instead, just looks at the loop names.

In the bottom portion of the Loop Browser there is a search field containing a little magnifying glass icon where you can enter search terms. Click in this field, type **funk**, and then press Return.

GarageBand then searches for loops that have names that contain the word you entered. For **funk**, there will be quite a few results. Typing **funk bass** will produce narrower results.

If you know a bit about music theory, you can also use the Scale pop-up menu to the left of the search field to narrow your results further. The options are Any, Minor, Major, Both, Neither, and Good for Both. But heck, the Beatles couldn't even read music and they did just fine.

CUSTOMIZING THE BUTTON VIEW

You can customize the buttons in the Loop Browser in many different ways. You can move the buttons around and even change the keywords they represent.

To move a button, simply drag it from its original location to the location of another button. When you drop it there, the two buttons swap.

To completely change the keyword that the button represents, hold the Control key down and click the button to bring up a complex pop-up menu of keyword choices. Then select the new keyword for the button to represent. Figure 2.5 shows the series of pull-down menus that you can use to select a new keyword for a button.

tip

In the Preferences dialog, which you can access by selecting GarageBand ···▷ Preferences, you will find a check box labeled Filter for More Relevant Results. When this is checked, the search results only include loops that are in a key close to your song's key. Uncheck the box to see more loop choices.

FIGURE 2.5
You can customize each button in the Loop Browser. Bongos, anyone?

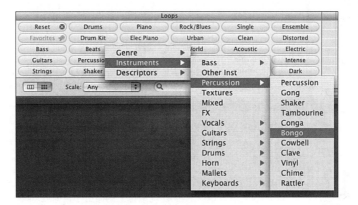

Changing the buttons is particularly useful if you are only interested in composing in a specific genre of music. For instance, if you like making hip-hop music, you probably don't need the Country button.

Moving and changing buttons is a great way to customize the Loop Browser to fit your style. You can replace keywords that you don't need with ones that make more sense for you. You can move the buttons around so you can group similar keywords together.

USING COLUMN VIEW

You can also browse for loops in column view. To get the column view, click the column view button at the bottom-left corner of the GarageBand window, as shown in Figure 2.6.

tip

You can reset the buttons to their default keywords and positions by selecting GarageBand ···▷ Preferences ···▷ General and clicking the Keyword Layout Reset button.

FIGURE 2.6
The Loop Browser is now in column view, which is simply an alternative way to find loops if you have an aversion to buttons.

Column View

Button View

Fav Check Boxes

> **caution**
>
> When you switch between column view and button view, the Loop Browser resets, so you lose any search criteria settings you have made so far.

> **tip**
>
> At lower monitor resolutions, the Loop Browser may not display all the loop information, such as Beats and Favorites, in the listing. Scroll the bottom window slider to the right to view the hidden information.

Now, the Loop Browser transforms into a column view similar to the column view in the OS X finder.

Figure 2.6 shows one way to navigate to the same three country drum loops we found before. We could have also looked in the Genres category and then selected Drums under that.

LOOP BROWSER FAVORITES

If you find yourself using the same loops over and over, you can tag them as Favorites. You do this by checking the Fav column check box in the loop list. The check boxes are shown in Figure 2.6 and are currently unchecked.

Anytime you want to view your favorite loops, just click Favorites whether you're in button or column view.

Using Favorites is a great way to narrow down your loop choices as you audition them. For instance, you can audition hundreds of loops and simply add ones that you like to your favorites. Then, when you have heard all the loops that fit your criteria, you can go back and listen to the ones in your favorites list again to find the best one.

AUDITIONING LOOPS

Whether you are using the button view or column view, the list of loops to the right side of the Loop Browser keeps the same format.

In addition to the name of the loop, you will see its native tempo, key, and number of beats. Here is what each column tells you about the loop:

* **Tempo**—This column indicates the native tempo of the loop. The tempo at which the loop is played corresponds to the tempo of your song. So, for instance, a loop with a tempo of 110 will be played slightly faster if your song is set to 120 beats per minute. This change is transparent to you, so if the loop sounds good in your song, you don't need to worry about what its original tempo was.

- **Key**—This column tells you about the scale, or group of notes, that the loop uses. Loops that use the same key, or keys that are nearby, will sound better together.
- **Beats**—This column shows the length of a loop in beats. For example, a 16-beat loop is four measures in length if the time signature is 4/4. This column allows you to determine the length of a loop in measures as long as you keep your time signature in mind.

Now it is time for the audition. To hear the loop play, simply click it in the list to the right. To stop it, click the loop again or click another loop.

The icon to the left of the loop name changes to a speaker icon when the loop begins to play. The loop repeats until you stop it or choose another loop.

TYPES OF LOOPS

There are two different types of icons that appear to the left of a loop name. One is a blue icon with a drawing of a sound wave. The other is a green icon with a musical note in it.

These icons represent the two different types of Apple Loops that GarageBand uses. The blue icon represents a Real Instrument loop. This is a prerecorded sound from a real instrument or group of instruments. It is basically a recorded sound.

The main difference between a Real Instrument loop and a sound that has been recorded with a microphone or other device is that Apple Loops have additional information in them to allow GarageBand to change the tempo and key of the sound. We'll look into making your own Real Instrument loops in Chapter 9, "Making Your Own Loops."

The other type of Apple Loop is called a Software Instrument loop. If you are familiar with MIDI files, you'll recognize a Software Instrument loop as a small piece of MIDI music.

A Software Instrument loop can act like a Real Instrument loop as well. If used as a Real Instrument loop by adding it to a track meant for Real Instrument loops, GarageBand converts the Software Instrument loop to an audio recording. If used as a Software Instrument loop, in a Software Instrument track, each note is generated on-the-fly as the song plays.

The main advantage of Software Instrument loops is that you can change the instrument that the loop uses without changing the actual notes in the loop. For instance, you can switch a loop from using a piano as its instrument to using a guitar.

The disadvantage to using Software Instrument loops is that they are processor intensive. So, if you are using a G3 Mac, or a low-end G4, you will find that adding more than one Software Instrument loop to your song may make it impossible for your Mac to play the song. A high-end G4 or G5 machine will be able to handle several Software Instrument loops.

The disadvantage of a Real Instrument loop is that you can't edit the notes. A Software Instrument loop can be changed, as we will see in Chapter 3.

In Chapter 9, we'll investigate how to make your own Software Instrument loops.

tip

There is no way to clear the favorites list quickly. But, you can uncheck the loops in your favorites list while viewing only your favorites.

note

In Figures 2.4 and 2.6, the key is not shown for the loops. This is because they are drum loops, which don't have a key. If these were piano or guitar loops, their keys would be displayed.

ADDING AND MODIFYING APPLE LOOPS

Once you have auditioned loops and have selected the one you want to use, adding the loop to your song is as easy as Mac users should expect. It is little more than a drag-and-drop process.

ADDING YOUR FIRST LOOP

To add a loop to your song, simply drag and drop the loop from the list in the Loop Browser to the empty timeline in the upper portion of the GarageBand window. Do this now with the Southern Beat 01 selected.

While dragging, notice some things that happen. First, the cursor changes to an interesting set of three elements: an arrow, a green circle with a plus symbol in it (indicates that you are adding a loop), and a text portion that shows the name of the loop.

When you move this cursor over the timeline, you see a vertical black line appear under the cursor as well. This snaps to a measure in the timeline to indicate where the loop will start. Make sure you drag the loop all the way over to the left, so the black line is at measure 1. This places your loop at the start of the song.

Once you release the mouse to complete the drag, there is a slight pause, and then the loop appears in the timeline. A track has been added to the timeline as shown in Figure 2.7.

FIGURE 2.7
The loop Southern Beat 01 has been added to the song and you won't even need to pay it royalties.

The Track column now contains the icon for the track and the name of the track for the loop you just added to it. In this case, it is called Drum Kit with a set of drums as the icon.

To listen to the music you just added to the timeline first click Go to Beginning, which is the leftmost button in the set of VCR-like controls. Then click Play in the same set of controls. These buttons are indicated in Figure 2.7.

What you should hear is the drum loop play through once and then stop. The red timeline indicator (called the playhead) continues, however, playing the silence at the end of the song. Click Stop to stop it.

EXTENDING THE LOOP

Apple Loops are called "loops" because they, well, loop! But so far, it only plays once in the song. To make the loop repeat, you need to extend the loop in the timeline to cover more space. For instance, if the drum loop is two measures long, you could stretch it to eight measures to have it repeat a total of four times.

To extend a loop, do the following:

1 Move your cursor over the right end of the loop. Notice that the cursor changes when it is there. If you are near the top part of the loop, it changes to a line with a curved arrow after it. If you are near the bottom of the loop, the cursor changes to a line with a straight arrow. Move your cursor around near the end of the loop to see both types of cursors.

2 To extend a loop, make sure the cursor shows the curved arrow and then click and drag the cursor to the right to extend the loop. Extend it to the start of measure 11, so that it looks like Figure 2.8.

FIGURE 2.8
The timeline now shows the loop extended over 10 measures. Nice to see it working so hard.

3 Click Go to Beginning and then Play; you hear the loop repeat five times.

You have laid the foundation of a short song.

ADDING A SECOND TRACK

Unless you're a drummer or really like drum solos, listening to one drum track isn't all that exciting. GarageBand's strength is being able to mix loops together. To do this, let's add a second track with another loop.

1 Use the Loop Browser in button mode.

2 Click the Bass button and then the Country button. You should see five loops appear in the Loop Browser list, all named Southern Bass.

3 Drag the first loop in the list to the timeline, just under the first track. Position the vertical black line so this second track starts at measure 3, instead of measure 1. This adds a second track to the timeline.

note

Notice that the vertical black line that moves with your cursor snaps to the nearest measure or fraction thereof. You can turn this off by selecting Control ····⟩ Snap to Grid. While learning GarageBand, it is best to leave this option on, which is the default.

4 Then drag the loop's end to extend all the way to the start of measure 11. See Figure 2.9 to see how the timeline should look now.

FIGURE 2.9
There are now two loops in two tracks. You've got a band!

To hear your song-in-the-making, click Go to Beginning and then Play. The song isn't much to listen to yet, but it's a start.

ADJUSTING TRACK VOLUME

Once you have several tracks in your song, you can easily turn them on and off. You can also adjust the volume of a track or your whole song at any point in the song.

MUTING AND SOLOING TRACKS

Now that we are playing with more than one track at a time, the song will start to get complex. As you continue to add tracks, you'll find the need to single out a track and temporarily silence it so you can concentrate on modifying other tracks.

The Tracks column has two buttons that allow you to temporarily silence tracks.

- **Mute**—This button, which looks like a speaker icon, allows you to silence the selected track when you engage it.
- **Solo**—This button, which looks like a headphones icon, silences all other tracks except the selected one when you engage it. This can also be toggled on or off.

Despite its name designation, you can solo more than one track at a time. If you solo one track, all other tracks are silenced. But if you engage another track's solo button, both soloed tracks are heard. The solo button takes precedence over any mute button when toggled on.

You can solo or mute any track at anytime—even during playback.

ADJUSTING TRACK VOLUME

While the Apple Loops are all made to work together, every Apple Loop doesn't work with every other one right off the bat. Sometimes you need to make simple changes, such as making a loop louder or quieter.

You can adjust the volume of an entire track using the volume slider in the Mixer column of the GarageBand window. You can do this while the song is stopped or while it is playing.

Lower the volume of the drum track and then play the song again.

You can also change where an instrument track appears within the stereo (left and right channels) field by adjusting the pan control (the dial marked with an L and R in the Mixer column). You can make the track play in only the left or right speaker or anywhere in between.

FADING A TRACK

Sometimes you may want to adjust the volume on just a portion of a track instead of the entire track. The most common example would be to have the track fade in at the beginning and then fade out at the end.

To do this, click the inverted triangle button, which is the rightmost button in the Tracks column for each track. It looks like a triangle pointing down.

What you get is another row under the track (see Figure 2.10).

FIGURE 2.10
After clicking the inverted triangle in the Mixer, the Track Volume expands under each track and allows you to control the volume of the track at any moment in the song.

The line in the track represents the volume curve. When you start, the volume curve is a straight line with a large dot at the left end. Checking the box next to Track Volume allows you to adjust this curve.

Playing with the volume curve is very simple. Click anywhere in it to create a new point that you can manipulate. Drag these points around to alter the curve. In Figure 2.11, three points have been added and moved around. The first dot starts the song off low, and then it raises to the volume level indicated by the second point. Then the third dot starts the fade-out to the fourth point.

FIGURE 2.11
By adjusting the volume curve, you can add a fade-in and fade-out. Now your tracks don't die; they just fade away.

THE MASTER TRACK

You can also adjust the volume of the entire song using the Master Track. The Master Track is a track that is always present in the song but is, by default, hidden. To make the master track visible, select Track ⟶ Show Master Track (⌘-B).

You can adjust the volume curve in the Master Track the same way you would do it for a single track. The only difference is that the volume changes are applied across all the tracks at the same time.

Figure 2.12 shows the Master Track and a simple fade-in and fade-out for the song.

FIGURE 2.12
The Master Track allows you to adjust the volume for the entire song.

WORKING WITH TRACKS AND REGIONS

Tracks are the main building blocks of GarageBand. To work effectively with GarageBand, you should know how to manipulate them and the elements inside them.

RENAMING REGIONS

The main element of a track is called a *region*. A region is a portion of track. It stretches from one measure to another in the track. You can have many regions in a track or only one.

In the previous figures, we have created two regions, one in the Drum Kit track and one in the Electric Bass track.

To bring up more information about a region, select it and choose Control ····⟩ Show Editor (⌘-E). You can also double-click the region to bring up the Editor.

The Editor replaces the Loop Browser at the bottom of the window as shown in Figure 2.13.

FIGURE 2.13
The Editor shows information about a region, including its name. Since this is a Software Instrument loop, you can see a complete set of notes arranged in a timeline.

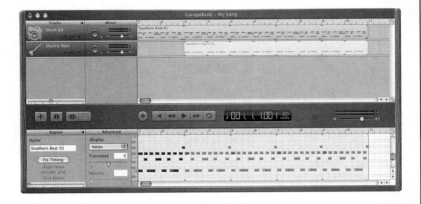

We'll learn more about the complete functionality of the Editor in Chapter 3. For now, it is enough to know that you can use it to change the name of the region. Just edit the name field to change it.

MOVING REGIONS

You can manipulate regions in all sorts of different ways. For instance, you have already learned how to stretch a region so that it loops several times.

In addition, you can move a region in its track of the timeline so that it starts at a specific time in the song. In Figure 2.13, the Southern Bass 01 region starts in measure 3. You can grab the region and move it earlier or later in the song.

SHORTENING A REGION

You can also shorten a region. Actually, you can do this in two ways. The first is to take a region that has been stretched to loop and shorten the loop. This is just more of the same manipulation that you used to lengthen the loop in the first place.

But you can also shorten each instance of the loop. To do this:

1 Start with a region that contains only one instance of the loop.

2 Grab the end of the loop at the bottom, when the cursor is a line with a straight arrow rather than a line with a curved arrow.

3 Drag the end of the loop forward or backward. Dragging it back shortens the loop, cutting off the end of it. Dragging it forward lengthens the loop, adding silence to the end.

For instance, if you shorten the loop halfway, you only get the first half of the loop. Then you can use the curved-arrow cursor to lengthen the loop again, which repeats only the first half of the loop rather than the whole thing.

Figure 2.14 shows what this can look like. It has two tracks. The first track contains `Ambient Beat 01` at full length, looped twice. The second track contains the same loop, but it was first shortened to only one measure long, cutting off the last three measures of the loop. Then it was stretched to cover the same eight measures as the region in the first track. The result is that the first measure of the loop is repeated eight times.

FIGURE 2.14
The timeline shows two regions using the same loop in different ways.

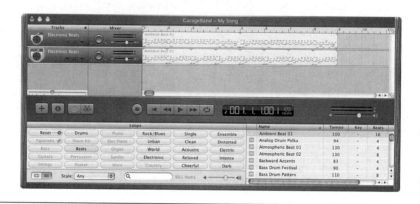

One of the great things about manipulating loop length is that you can also do it after you have stretched the region.

Say you have a loop that is 2 measures long and is stretched to through the 10th measure. So, it loops 5 times. You can shorten the loop length to 1 measure, cutting off the second half of the loop. The region remains 10 measures long, so the loop now repeats 10 times across the 10 measures.

All you need to do is place the cursor near the end of the first instance of the loop, near the bottom of the track, and you will get the straight-arrow cursor again. Then you can change the loop segment's length. This will then be reflected throughout the loop.

It is hard to understand this without trying it for yourself, so go ahead and drop a loop into a track. Then use the curved-arrow cursor to drag the end of it to expand the region to loop several times. Now go back to the end of the first instance of the loop in the region and shrink it. You will see the loop tighten up throughout the length of the region.

SPLITTING A REGION

Changing the loop length is just one way you can take an Apple Loop and change it to fit your composition. You can also take a region of a song and split it into two.

For instance, if you have an Apple Loop stretched to repeat over 10 measures, you can split the loop so it repeats over the first 5 measures, then skips 2 measures, and then repeats for a second group of 5 measures.

To do this, you must move the playhead at the top of the timeline. Simply drag it so that the playhead, and the red line connected to it, are at the spot in the region where you want to split it.

Then, select Edit ---> Split (⌘-T). You won't see much of a change to start, except that the name of the region is now duplicated starting at your split point and a line intersects the region. But you can now drag the first and second regions independently.

Figure 2.15 shows what happens when you split a region and then move the second region away from the first to create a few measures of silence.

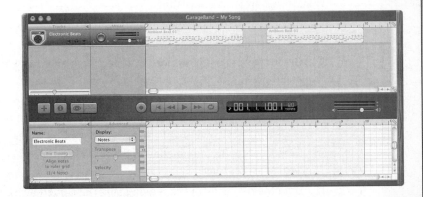

FIGURE 2.15
A single region was split in two and moved to create a break between them.

ADVANCED REGION MANIPULATION

You can pretty much manipulate regions as you like using the Split command and simple drag-and-drop motions. You can also copy, cut, and paste regions with the standard menu commands that all Mac applications use in the Edit menu.

While you could drag and drop the same Apple Loop from the Loop Browser several times, being able to copy and paste regions can be easier. For instance, if you have several regions over several tracks, it would be easier to copy and paste the regions than to find the loops again. You can then change the second copies to vary your song.

Once you have split regions, you can rejoin them with the Edit ---> Join Selected command (⌘-J). However, this also resets the region's loop length, which also expands the region's length according to the number of times the region loops. It is very easy to create a mess when joining selected regions.

In many cases, it will be better to rebuild a region from scratch or extend it from the first segment of a previously split region.

tip

You don't have to rely strictly on Apple Loops to make your song, however. You can also import original content stored as audio files, as you'll learn in subsequent chapters.

CREATING A DANCE SONG

Building a song is a creative process. Thanks to GarageBand, you get to decide how many tracks you want, what the tracks are, and every other detail.

So far in this chapter, we have been building a country/southern rock song as an example. You can take what you've learned so far and add more tracks to the song to finish it off. How complex the song gets will depend on your needs. For instance, a simple two-track song will be fine for background music for a home video or a piece of multimedia software, even a Web site. But if you want to play the song as a standalone tune to enjoy, you will probably want to add a whole lot more.

Now that you've gotten your feet wet, let's use what you have learned to create a simple electronic dance song.

LAYING DOWN THE DRUMS

First, let's start with a new song:

1   Select File ⋯⟩ New (or you can press ⌘-N) and then accept the default settings and give your song a unique name.

2   Delete the Grand Piano track by selecting it and pressing ⌘-Delete. Now you have an empty song that we can add some Apple Loops to.

3   First, let's find a good drum track. Open the Loop Browser and click the Beats button and Electronic button to narrow down the number of loops displayed. Then scan down the list and look for Deep House Dance Beat 01.

4   Drag this loop to the timeline in the first measure. You end up with a region that is two measures long.

5   Drag the right side of the region using the curved-arrow cursor to extend the loop to the right. Drag it all the way to the other side of the screen and let the timeline scroll automatically to the right. Extend it to 40 measures, stopping at the start of measure 41. Figure 2.16 shows the GarageBand window just after the loop has been extended.

FIGURE 2.16
The Deep House Dance Beat 01 region has been extended for 40 measures. That should keep the kids jumpin'.

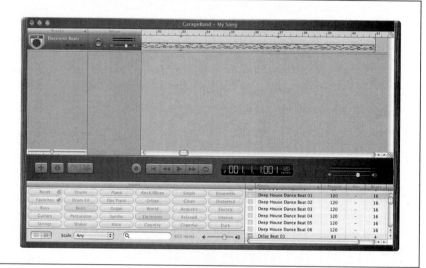

You can test out the song by clicking Go to Beginning and then clicking Play. There's not much point to doing that now, except that you get a chance to listen to the loop again in preparation for selecting another loop that will go well with it.

LAYING DOWN THE BASS

Next, let's select a bass loop:

1 Click Reset in the Loop Browser and then select the Bass and Electronic buttons. The first loop in the list should be the `80s Dance Bass Synth 01` loop.

2 Scroll the timeline back to the first measure and drag that to the empty area below track 1. Make sure that the region starts at the very left.

3 Then, stretch it to the same 40-measure length as the first track.

4 Now click Go to Beginning and Play to hear the mix of the two tracks. They go together well and create a pretty basic background for our dance song.

LAYING DOWN THE MELODY

Now let's add some more tracks to the song:

1 Reset the Loop Browser and click Synth and Cheerful. The first loop should be `80s Dance Bass Synth 06`.

2 Add that as another track by dragging it to the empty space in the timeline.

3 Instead of repeating this loop over the entire length of the song, drag the loop to start in the third measure and stretch it for four measures until measure 6.

4 Then copy and paste the region and put it again in measures 9–12. You do this by performing the copy and then clicking the measure ruler at the top of the timeline to set the playhead at measure 9. Then you paste.

The result looks like Figure 2.17. The third track, marked `Synthesizer`, has two regions in it. Play the song from the beginning now to hear what you have so far.

FIGURE 2.17
The first two tracks are background, and the third is a sort of melody. At least it will pass for one in a dance song.

Now let's add some horn:

1   Reset the Loop Browser and click the Horn button. Then scroll down and find RnB Horn Section 07.

2   Add it in a new track, starting at measure 7. Then shorten the length of the region to only one measure. This cuts off most of the loop, leaving just the start of it.

3   Copy and paste this region into measure 13. But this time expand the region back to its original loop length of three measures so that the entire loop plays through once. Figure 2.18 shows these two regions in the timeline.

FIGURE 2.18
The RnB Horn Section 07 is used twice, with the first region only allowing the very beginning of the loop to play.

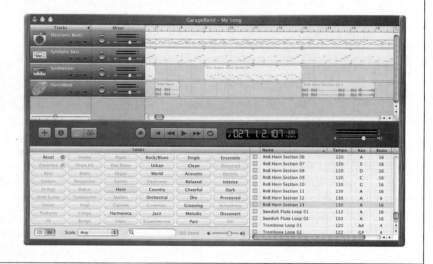

This fourth track, named Horn/Wind, is a Real Instrument track. That means that the regions in it are loops using real audio files, not MIDI-like Apple Loops.

We can add another horn region to this same track later in the song. Find the loop RnB Horn Section 13 and place it starting at measure 21. Then also copy and paste the bass regions in the third track, Synthesizer, so they appear again at measures 17 and 25. Figure 2.19 shows all these changes.

FIGURE 2.19
Create a region of RnB Horn Section 13 at measure 21, and repeat the bass regions a few more times to keep it funky.

Now let's go back to the `RnB Horn Section 07` region and make two more copies of it to end this short song. Make a new region that will stretch from measures 30 to 36 and will repeat only the very start of the loop. Make one more region that will be the entire loop and start immediately after at measure 37. You can see this final piece of the song in Figure 2.20.

FIGURE 2.20
The song ends by repeating the main horn melody one last time and then letting the synth track echo away. The kids love that sort of stuff.

In addition to the horn track, we'll place a short reprise of the `80s Dance Bass Synth 06` at the very end. It will be the only track playing for that last measure. The track has an echo quality to it, which sounds nice when it is isolated like this.

This completes the song. You can find a copy of the song file at the Web site `http://macaudioguy.com/gbb/downloads/`.

EXTENDING THE SONG

And there you have it, a simple electronic dance song done with only Apple Loops and a little region manipulation. Be sure to save this song for future reference, and so that all your hard work isn't lost.

But you don't have to stop here. You can continue to add tracks or modify them. In upcoming chapters, you will find out how to change the track instruments, record your own tracks, export your finished song to iTunes, and burn your own CD to play for your adoring fans.

3

RECORDING YOUR OWN MUSIC WITH SOFTWARE INSTRUMENTS

No doubt that playing around with the prerecorded Apple Loops is fun. But the real power of GarageBand is creating your own musical compositions with Software Instruments. Let's unleash the power to create your own compositions using GarageBand's Software Instruments.

PLAYING GARAGEBAND'S SOFTWARE INSTRUMENTS

Perhaps the coolest thing about GarageBand is that for your $49, you get over 50 great-sounding instruments with it. You get practically an entire orchestra inside your Mac. Previously, when you bought a MIDI sequencer you either had to buy add-on Virtual Instrument packages costing hundreds of dollars or have MIDI hardware sound modules hooked into your Mac. No more, thanks to GarageBand.

Let's find out just what Software Instruments are. Also, how you can use either GarageBand's onscreen Musical Keyboard or a MIDI keyboard to play music with Software Instruments.

WHAT ARE SOFTWARE INSTRUMENTS?

In GarageBand there are two kinds of instruments.

- Prerecorded sound files (such as Apple Loops and imported sound files) or a live audio input (such as a guitar or vocals) plus any effects added to them to form a RealInstrument.

- Sounds generated within GarageBand plus any effects added to them form a Software Instrument.

notes

Refer to Chapter 1, "Getting Started with GarageBand," when using Software Instruments to make sure you have your system set for optimal performance.

You can learn more about exporting your song to iTunes in Chapter 7, "Finishing Up."

GarageBand calls these built-in sound generators Software Instruments. The important thing to know is that you can play Software Instruments in GarageBand with GarageBand's Onscreen Musical Keyboard or an external MIDI keyboard.

Another thing about Software Instruments is that they use your Mac's processor to do some very complex calculations to generate sound, so the more powerful your Mac is, the more software instruments you can use at any one time. Before we actually start to play these things, let's find out a little more about MIDI.

WHAT IS MIDI?

Back in the early '80s someone thought it would be a great idea if they could use one keyboard to control a whole stack of synthesizers. *Musical Instrument Digital Interface (MIDI)* was born. MIDI is a language that allows a controller musical instrument to talk to a bunch of other instruments—much the same way your keyboard talks to your Mac.

Someone else figured out that you could record those musical instructions and save them to a file. Then, you could play that file back and control not only the original stack of synthesizers, but also any stack of MIDI-compatible instruments that you wanted.

The MIDI sequencer was born. This is exactly the same as if you typed a document into your Mac and later decided you wanted to change the font. So think of a MIDI sequencer as a musical word processor.

GarageBand is a MIDI sequencer in addition to being a loop sequencer and audio recorder. The only difference between GarageBand and a high-end MIDI sequencer is that GarageBand can't export a MIDI file of your performances for use in other programs. It can, however, use its built-in Software Instruments to play back your performance and save it in the GarageBand song file. You can also export your song as an audio file to iTunes.

PLAYING SOFTWARE INSTRUMENTS USING THE ONSCREEN MUSICAL KEYBOARD

As a special bonus, Apple has included a handy onscreen music keyboard with GarageBand. Let's play with it!

Launch GarageBand. If this is the first time you have used GarageBand, the New Project dialog appears immediately. Otherwise, you can bring up the New Project dialog by selecting File ⟶ New.

Go ahead and accept the settings and click Create. If a dialog comes up that asks you if you would like to replace the project My Song, click Replace (unless you have already created a masterpiece using that filename, in which case you need to give the new file a unique name).

You should now be looking at a screen that is similar to the one shown in Figure 3.1. You might also already have the Onscreen Musical Keyboard window labeled Grand Piano open; if not, select Window, Keyboard (or just press ⌘+K).

FIGURE 3.1
This is GarageBand's default New Song screen. But wait, there's more! GarageBand also includes the free Grand Piano bonus track.

Now you should definitely have the Onscreen Musical Keyboard floating in front of the main GarageBand window. The keyboard will look very much like what you see in Figure 3.2.

FIGURE 3.2
It's the Onscreen Musical Keyboard, with real musical keyboard action!

Click the Onscreen Musical Keyboard key labeled C4. You should see the key turn blue and hear the glorious tone of the GarageBand Grand Piano sounding the note middle C.

Now click several times on the C4 key, starting at the bottom of the key and working upward toward the top of the key. Notice how the sound is softer toward the top and louder toward the bottom. This is Apple's clever solution to being able to play dynamically using the Onscreen Musical Keyboard.

Go ahead and try clicking to play the keys. Fun, huh? Notice that you can click the little arrows on the left and right of the Onscreen Musical Keyboard. These arrows move the keyboard range up or down an octave. Wow! Even more fun, click and drag across the keys and you can be a virtual Jerry Lee Lewis!

Playing a 1'' tall piano has its appeal, but let's turn it up a notch. Select Track, Show Track Info (or press ⌘-I) . In the Track Info window select Guitars and then Big Electric Lead. Close the Track Info window. Notice that, in the Tracks column of the main GarageBand window, the Grand Piano has

tip
Click the green window button in the upper-left corner of the Onscreen Musical Keyboard. Holy ebony and ivory, Batman! It's the world's longest keyboard! Click the green button again and your keyboard returns to normal size. You can also drag the lower-right corner of the window to expand the keyboard horizontally.

turned into Big Electric Lead. Also notice that your Onscreen Musical Keyboard is now labeled Big Electric Lead. Go ahead and jam a little—or a lot.

Okay, enough! Select Track, Show Track Info again. In the Track Info window, select Drum Kits and then Dance Kit. Close the Track Info window. Notice that, in the Tracks column of the main GarageBand window, the Big Electric Lead has turned into Dance Kit (see Figure 3.3). Also notice that your Onscreen Musical Keyboard is now labeled Dance Kit.

Click the Onscreen Musical Keyboard key labeled C1. If you can't see the key labeled C1, shift the keyboard an octave down using the arrow button on the left side of the Onscreen Musical Keyboard. When you click C1, you should hear a kick drum; if you move up one white key to D1, it should sound like a snare drum.

Explore where various drums are on the keyboard. This is known as the *drum key map*. Refer to Appendix H, "General MIDI Drum Key Map," for a drum key map diagram.

FIGURE 3.3
The Onscreen Musical Keyboard has magically changed its name and sound from a grand piano to a lead guitar to a dance drum kit.

Select GarageBand, Quit GarageBand (or press ⌘-Q), and then click Don't Save.

Next we'll talk about using an external MIDI music keyboard. If you don't have a MIDI keyboard yet, you can still use the Onscreen Musical Keyboard in the rest of this chapter's exercises, but using a full-size keyboard sure will be easier.

Using a full-size musical keyboard is vastly superior to using GarageBand's Onscreen Musical Keyboard to play and record music in GarageBand. But it's nice to know that the onscreen keyboard is there if you need it.

RECORDING A SOFTWARE INSTRUMENT TRACK

tip

If you have a USB music keyboard, just plug it into your Mac. If you have a MIDI model (one that only supports a 5-pin connector), you need a USB MIDI interface to bridge your gear to your Mac. Refer to "Hooking Up Your MIDI keyboard" in Appendix B, "Configuring Your Studio."

While being able to play GarageBand's Software Instruments is fun in a "Let's all gather around the piano" sort of way, the real meat and potatoes of GarageBand is its recording capabilities. You learned how to lay down a rhythm track using Apple Loops in Chapter 2, "Making Music with Apple Loops." Now you'll learn how to lay down some tracks of your own.

THE GARAGEBAND CONTROL BAR

You can control most of GarageBand's recording functions from the Control Bar.

Let's take a quick tour of the Control Bar's buttons and functions. Your homework for tonight is to memorize Figure 3.4.

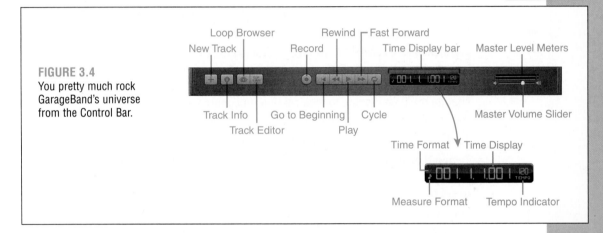

FIGURE 3.4
You pretty much rock GarageBand's universe from the Control Bar.

Starting from the left side of the bar, the buttons and controls are as follows:

- **New Track**—This button brings up the New Track window. You can also go to the Track menu and select New Track (or press Option-⌘-N). The New track window allows you to create a new track and select an instrument in GarageBand's main window.

- **Track Info**—This button brings up the Track Info window. You can also go to the Track menu and select Show Track Info (or press ⌘-I). The Track Info window allows you to select a new instrument for the currently selected track.

- **Loop Browser**—Use this button to open the Loop Browser panel. You can also go to the Control menu and select Show Loop Browser (or press ⌘-L). The Loop Browser is covered in depth in Chapter 2.

- **Track Editor**—The Track Edit panel opens when you click this button. You can also go to the Control menu and select Show Editor (⌘-E). The Track Editor is covered in depth later in this chapter.

- **Record button**—Clicking this button (or pressing R on your keyboard) toggles the record function on and off. Click to start recording and then click again to stop.
- **Go to Beginning**—Clicking this button (or pressing the Home or Z key) returns the playhead to the beginning of the song.
- **Rewind**—As its clever name indicates, clicking this button (or pressing the left-arrow key) moves the playhead backward one measure. It rewinds the playhead if clicked and held.
- **Play**—Clicking this button (or pressing the spacebar) toggles between the play/pause function.
- **Fast Forward**—If you guessed that this button (or pressing the right-arrow key) moves the playhead forward one measure when clicked or fast-forwards the playhead if clicked and held, then you were exactly right.
- **Cycle**—Click this button (or press the C key) to toggle the cycle region function. The cycle function allows you to cycle (loop) a section of a song for either recording or playback.
- **Time Display bar**—Contains the Time and Tempo Display as well as the MIDI Input Indicator.
- **Time/Measure Format**—Clicking this button toggles the format of the time display. To change the time display to absolute time (hours, minutes, seconds, and fractions of a second), click the small clock button to the upper left of the display. To change the time display to musical time (measures, beats, and beat divisions), click the small note button to the lower left of the display.
- **Time Display**—This area shows the current location of the playhead.
- **Tempo Indicator**—Here you can change the tempo of your song. To change the tempo of your song, click the tempo in the display and drag the slider that appears to set a new tempo.
- **Master Level Meters**—Displays the overall output volume level of a song.
- **Master Volume Slider**—Drag to adjust the overall output volume level of a song.

Familiarizing yourself with the buttons and controls of the Control Bar will make working with GarageBand much easier. Next we'll explore actually recording a Software Instrument track.

RECORDING YOUR FIRST SOFTWARE INSTRUMENT TRACK

Now that you've played Software Instruments using a keyboard and had a quick run-through on GarageBand's buttons and controls, you are ready to record a Software Instrument track. We'll also familiarize you with some more of GarageBand's interface elements and controls.

Let's go ahead launch GarageBand and open a new song:

1. If this is the first time you have used GarageBand, the New Project dialog appears immediately. Otherwise, you can bring up the New Project dialog by selecting File ····⟩ New.

2. Go ahead and accept the Tempo and Key settings, name the song `Key test`, and click Create.

3   We should pretty much be looking at the same screen as we had in Figure 3.1 with Grand Piano as the selected Software Instrument. If you are using a MIDI keyboard, play a few notes to make sure that your MIDI keyboard is connected correctly.

4   Select Control ····⟩ Metronome if you want to hear a metronome to help you play on tempo. Selecting Control ····⟩ Count In gives you a one-measure count-in before recording. This is just like Joey Ramone counting in before every song, except you don't hear Joey shouting, "One, two, tree, fo'!"

5   Click Record. You should hear a clicking sound—that is the metronome. Notice that the first click for every measure is slightly louder and at a different pitch. This helps you to begin to play at the beginning of a measure.

6   Play a few notes; then click Play to pause the playhead, and stop recording. Notice that a green region named Grand Piano has been created in the timeline.

If you would like to play back what you just recorded, click Go to Beginning and then click Play. You should see the playhead move along the timeline. When the playhead reaches the segment, you should hear the notes that you recorded.

Click Play or press the spacebar on your computer keyboard to pause playback. Then click Go to Beginning to return to the beginning of your song. This should look something like Figure 3.5.

FIGURE 3.5
Look, Mom, my first
GarageBand recording!

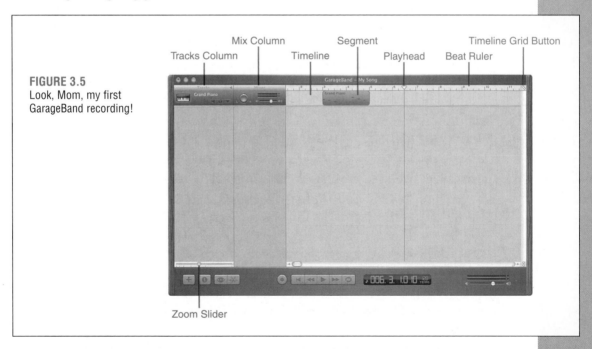

Congratulations, you've completed your first GarageBand Software Instrument recording. Unless you are particularly attached to your recording, you can now delete the region you just recorded by either going to the Edit menu and selecting Delete or pressing the Delete key on your computer keyboard.

Let's take a quick tour of some the features of the Track window as shown in Figure 3.5. There will be a pop quiz:

- **Tracks column**—Contains the name and icon for an instrument as well as the Mute button, which silences the track; the Solo button, which allows you to hear a track by itself; and the Track Volume disclosure triangle, which shows the track's volume curve in the timeline.

- **Mix column**—Contains the Pan wheel, which allows you to adjust the left-right positioning of a track in the stereo field; the Volume slider, which adjust the track's volume during recording and playback; and the level meters, which allow you to see the track's volume level.

- **Zoom slider**—Drag the Zoom slider to see a closer view or to view more of the timeline.

- **Region**—Regions are created when you add loops or record Software or Real Instruments. You can cut, copy, paste, and otherwise manipulate regions to build the arrangement of your song.

- **Timeline**—The area that contains your recorded tracks and regions as well as the beat ruler, which acts as a time-based ruler for your song. The timeline is where you arrange your song.

- **Playhead**—Shows the current position in the song that is being played or recorded. You can also move the playhead to navigate through the song.

- **Beat ruler**—A time-based ruler that is subdivided by measures and beats, which are the units of musical time. You can click the beat ruler to move the playhead to a precise position on the timeline.

- **Timeline grid button**—Adjusts the resolution of the beat ruler. Set it to automatic to have the value change as you zoom in or out in the timeline.

CYCLE RECORDING A SOFTWARE INSTRUMENT TRACK

Cycle recording is a powerful method for recording Software Instruments in GarageBand. We'll show you how to build up a drum loop using cycle recording.

We are going to presume that you still have your song, aptly titled Key test, still open. If not, the rest of the class will wait around while you open the song.

Just to make things more interesting, let's build a four-measure drum loop. First let's switch the Software Instrument from Grand Piano to the Pop Drum kit:

1 Select Control ⤑ Metronome to keep us on beat.

2 Select Track ⤑ Track Info. In the Track Info window select Drum Kits and then Pop Kit.

3 Close the Track Info window, and you should have Pop Kit as the current instrument.

4 Click Cycle. You will notice that a yellow bar appears below the beat ruler of the timeline. This is called the cycle region (see Figure 3.6).

5 Drag the cycle region so that it is between measures 1 and 5 on the timeline. Click Record and play a few notes in time with the metronome with your keyboard.

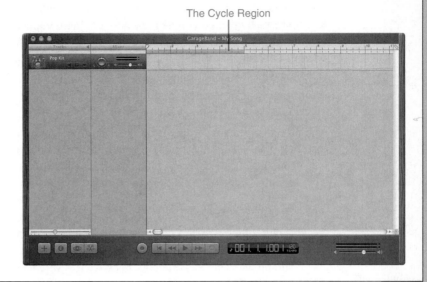

The Cycle Region

FIGURE 3.6
The cycle region is sort of like GarageBand's spin cycle.

6 Notice that you have created a four-measure region that is cycling and that the Record button is still active.

7 While still recording, play a few more notes. The new notes are added to your previously played notes. While the notes displayed in the region seem to be erased with each pass of the cycle, you can still hear all the notes that you have played.

8 Click Record to toggle the recording off. Notice that GarageBand is continuing to play back the cycle region and that now all the notes that you played are displayed in the region.

9 Click Play to pause playback.

You can see how cycle recording is really useful if you want to create a complex melody but can only hen-peck keys or are using the onscreen keyboard.

Play and record a few notes on the first pass of the cycle region, and you can add notes one or more at a time each time the region cycles. GarageBand keeps adding your performances to the existing notes. Click the record button or press the R key when you're finished and want to stop recording.

Click Record again. Play some more notes. Notice that your notes are being appended to the previous recording. Click Record to toggle the recording off. Your region with all the appended notes will continue to play. Go ahead and click Play to pause playback.

You can add notes to a previously recorded Software Instrument region. Cool, huh?

caution

Exiting the cycle recording using the record button appends each recording cycle. Exiting the Cycle Record mode using the play button keeps only the last recording cycle, discarding the previously recorded cycles.

I'm going to repeat the caution I already offered on the side—it is really, really important. If you exit cycle recording by clicking the play button or you press the spacebar to stop recording when you have cycling enabled, you will lose all of your previous recordings—only your last recording pass will have been saved. This feature is both powerful and dangerous.

For example, if you want to play a part over and over until you get it just right, exit cycle recording by clicking the play button or pressing the spacebar to stop recording and only your last and presumably best pass will be saved.

Also note that cycle recording is not just for drums. Cycle recording any Software Instrument works exactly the same way whether the Software Instrument is drums or acoustic guitar—as long as it is a Software Instrument. As you will see in the next chapter, cycle recording works differently for Real Instruments.

OVERDUBBING A SECTION OF A RECORDING

note

You can also overdub a section of a recording by creating another track with the same instrument of the track you wish to overdub. Use cycle recording to record your new notes and edit the regions to append or replace the offending notes. This is a safer but more processor-intensive method.

Overdubbing a region using cycle recording is a two-edged axe that will allow you to either append or replace notes within a Software Instrument region. But be careful with that axe, Eugene, because it is very easy to replace when you intend to append.

Say that we really liked three out of four measures of our previously recorded four-measure drum region and that we want to append or replace some notes to measure 2. You can use cycle recording to overdub a portion of a Software Instrument region either to append or replace notes, depending on how you exit cycle recording. Take another glance at the caution in the previous section, so we don't want to have to say, "Told you so."

Go up to the yellow Cycle Segment bar with your cursor. Notice that as you roll over the ends of the Cycle Segment bar that your cursor changes to a vertical bar with left or a right arrow. You can click and drag either end of the cycle region to make it larger or smaller. Use this method to place the cycle segment over measure 2 of your song, as shown in Figure 3.7.

FIGURE 3.7
Honey, I've shrunk the cycle region.

Click Record. Play a couple more notes. To append the notes to your recording, click Record again to exit the Recording mode. You should hear your appended notes playing back. To replace the notes of the cycle region, click Play to exit Recording mode. Click Play again and you should only hear your newly recorded notes. Click Play to pause playback. And then click Cycle to turn off cycling.

You now have a new highlighted region on measure 2 with either the appended or replaced notes. Shift-click the measure 1 region and the measure 3 and 4 regions. You should have all the regions highlighted at this point. Go to the Edit menu and select Join Selected. This command merges the data of all the selected regions and creates a single region with the appended or replaced notes in measure 2.

If you are not happy with the replaced segment, you have one last opportunity to undo your recording. Go to the Edit menu and select Undo Recording to give it another shot.

EDITING A SOFTWARE INSTRUMENT TRACK

The biggest plus to recording Software Instruments is that they can be edited extensively after recording. After recording a track, not only can you change the sound of an instrument, but you can change the entire instrument. You can see if that screaming guitar solo sounds better as a screaming sax solo or even a screaming tuba solo if you happen to be touring Wisconsin.

You also have extensive note editing options to make sure that your recording of "The Depeche Mode Polka" comes out just right.

EDITING SOFTWARE INSTRUMENT REGIONS

Editing and manipulating Software Instrument regions is exactly the same as manipulating Software Instrument loops, which we did in Chapter 2.

CHANGING SOFTWARE INSTRUMENTS

After you've recorded a track with one Software Instrument, you can easily switch the track to another Software Instrument to see how it might sound. Let's record a new four-measure cycle:

1 Create a new song by selecting File ⸺⧽ New.

2 Accept the Tempo and Key settings. Name the song `Change test`. Click Create.

3 Click Cycle and expand the cycle region to cover measures 1–4.

4 Click Record and play some notes; then click Record again to turn recording off. You should hear the notes that you recorded playing back and cycling over and over and over. Starting to get tired of the Grand Piano?

5 Select Track ⸺⧽ Track Info. In the Track Info window select Strings and Hollywood Strings. After a couple of seconds, you will hear that the instrument has indeed changed to Hollywood Strings. Close the Track Info window to accept the change.

6 Click Play to pause playback. Your piano part has now become a string part.

You will notice, however, that the track region is still labeled Grand Piano; this is handy if you want to remember which instrument you used to originally record a part. You can just as easily rename the region to the new instrument or anything else for that matter. Renaming regions is a perfect segue to our next section on using the Track Editor.

EDITING SOFTWARE INSTRUMENT TRACKS USING THE TRACK EDITOR

GarageBand's Track Editor allows you to edit almost everything in a Software Instrument track region. Using the Track Editor, you can often turn that so-so performance into something special.

Like cracking a nut, there are several ways to open the Track Editor. If you are into clicking buttons, click the track editor button on the GarageBand Control Bar (refer to Figure 3.4). You can also go to the Track menu and select Show Editor (or press ⌘-E). Or you can even double-click a region in the timeline to open that region in the Track Editor (see Figure 3.8).

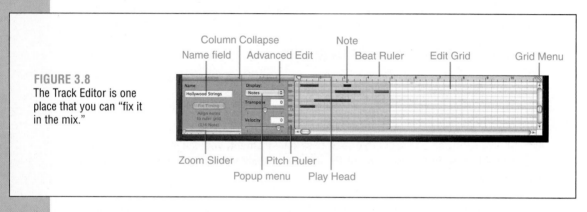

FIGURE 3.8
The Track Editor is one place that you can "fix it in the mix."

RENAMING A REGION

To rename a region, simply click in the Name field and type in a new name.

FIXING NOTE TIMING

Even if you were not playing exactly on the beat, you can use the magic of the Fix Timing button to put you in the pocket. The Fix Timing button snaps your notes to the nearest ruler grid as defined by the Grid menu setting. The Grid menu is that small ruler icon hiding out in upper-right corner of the Track Editor (refer to Figure 3.8). Clicking the Grid menu brings up a menu of various musical timing divisions as well as an automatic setting (see Figure 3.9). The automatic setting is tied to the Zoom slider setting in the lower-left corner of the Track Editor (refer to Figure 3.8).

To fix a region's timing, you must first highlight the region by clicking the region in the Edit Timeline grid. Then set the beat amount you want your notes to snap to by either moving the Zoom slider or selecting a value from the Grid menu. And then finally snap your notes to a grid value by clicking the Fix Timing button. Experiment with different timing values to get your region's rhythm to sound just right.

FIGURE 3.9
The Grid menu, like
Frodo's ring, is small and
very powerful.

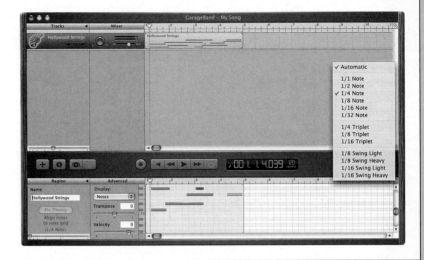

You can also alter a note's timing by clicking the note in the Edit grid and moving the note by click-dragging the note left or right on the grid. And, again, you can adjust the grid timing values by either moving the Zoom slider or selecting a value from the Grid menu.

For many, the Fix Timing button is a godsend as it can correct small mistakes in timing; for others it is hell spawned because it can easily ruin subtle intentional nuances in timing. Use it at your own risk. There's always Undo.

CHANGING A REGION'S PITCH

If you played a region in a different musical key from the rest of the song or would just like to hear a part in a different key, you can adjust the pitch of the entire region by moving the Transpose slider. Note that the pitch values of the notes on the Edit grid do not change with the Transpose value. The notes on the Edit grid remain at their original positions on the grid. Only the Transpose display tells you that the notes have been transposed.

EDITING A NOTE'S LOUDNESS

A particular note's loudness is determined by its velocity value. The harder you play a note the louder it is. You can adjust the overall loudness of a region by selecting all the notes in a region (press ⌘-A) and adjusting the Velocity slider. You can also select an individual note and adjust its velocity value with the Velocity slider.

tip

You can introduce chordal movement into your song by duplicating a region a couple of times and then transposing the duplicated regions. A classic "Louie, Louie" rock-and-roll chord movement is CCC, FF, GGG, FF.

note

Velocity doesn't just affect loudness; it can also affect the character of a note. Some Software Instruments sound quite different depending on how loudly or softly they are played.

tip

You can select a group of notes to edit by Shift-clicking them or by dragging around the group of notes. You can then perform any of the previously mentioned editing functions to the group of notes, as well as the standard Mac edit functions of cut, copy, paste, and delete.

EDITING NOTE PITCH

If you hit a wrong note when recording a region, don't worry. You can fix it in the editor. You can alter a particular note's pitch by clicking the note in the Edit grid and moving the note by click-dragging the note up or down on the grid. Notice that you hear the note's pitch change as you move it up or down on the grid. Also note the piano keyboard–like ruler on left side of the grid to help you find the pitch you are looking for.

EDITING NOTE DURATION

Sometimes a note is held down too long or not long enough. This is called the note's *duration*. You can alter a particular note's duration by clicking and dragging the tail end of the note forward or backward in the Edit grid. If Snap To Grid is enabled in the Control menu, the note's duration snaps to the grid value as set in the Grid menu or by the Zoom slider.

DUPLICATING AND ADDING NOTES

Not only can you fix mistakes in the editor, but you can also get creative. If you want to duplicate a note and then drag it to another pitch or place in the timeline, just select the note you wish to duplicate and drag it to another location while holding down the Option key. If you want to add a note to the region, press ⌘ and you'll see the cursor change to a pencil shape. Place the cursor over the point in the grid where you want the note to appear and then click to place the note.

EDITING MODULATION, PITCH BEND, AND SUSTAIN

Modulation, pitch bend, and sustain are ways to add musical expression to notes beyond pitch, loudness, and duration. These are known in the MIDI world as *continuous controllers*. Your MIDI keyboard probably has a pitch bend and a modulation wheel as well as a jack for a sustain pedal. You might use the pitch bend wheel to "bend" a note in a sax solo, the modulation wheel to add vibrato to a cello, or the sustain pedal to extend the sound of a piano note.

If you recorded your performance and used these controllers, you have the ability to edit them in the Edit window. Click the Display pop-up menu to select either Pitch Bend, Modulation, or Sustain:

- **Pitch bend**—Can alter the pitch of a note or series of notes up or down two semitones for most Software Instruments. These are expressed in GarageBand's editor as grid values between –64 and +64.

- **Modulation**—Usually controls the vibrato or rapid cyclic volume modulation of a note or notes of a Software Instrument. These are expressed in GarageBand's editor as grid values between 0 and 127, depending on the depth of modulation.

- **Sustain**—An on or off value, it is expressed in GarageBand's editor as grid values between 0 and 1, with 1 meaning that sustain is on.

You can experiment with altering these values in a previously recorded performance or edit the values in the Track Editor if you used these controllers while recording a Software Instrument.

If the controller was used, the controller's movements appear as lines connected by dots, called *control points*. These are similar to a volume curve in the timeline, which we explored in the "Adjusting Track Volume" section of Chapter 2 (see Figure 3.10).

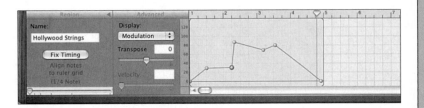

FIGURE 3.10
A modulation curve that looks strangely like my stock portfolio's value.

You can move the control points on the grid to change their values or click the line to add a control point. You can also use ⌘-click to draw control points from scratch. Select a control and press Delete to delete a control point.

caution

Using continuous controllers adds a huge amount of data to the MIDI stream, which may negatively affect GarageBand's performance. Use continuous controllers judiciously and use the editor to thin the control points.

EDITING SOFTWARE INSTRUMENTS

GarageBand has a great collection of Software Instruments, but there is going to come a time when you want to tweak an instrument to make it sound just right, or you might even want to perform massive surgery on an instrument to give it a sound all your own. We will go into depth about creating your instruments in Chapter 8, "Making Your Own Software and Real Instruments." But for now we'll show you how to alter a Software Instrument and save it as part of your song.

SOFTWARE INSTRUMENT SETTINGS

If you open the Track Info window, you will notice a triangle marked Details... in the lower-left corner of the window. If you click that triangle, suddenly the Track Info window expands and you can find all the settings which make each Software Instrument unique. Take a look at Figure 3.11.

THE TWO PARTS OF A SOFTWARE INSTRUMENT: GENERATORS AND EFFECTS

There are basically two parts that make up a Software Instrument: a generator, which creates the instrument's sound, and effects, which alter the instrument's sound.

The main difference between a Software Instrument and a Real Instrument in GarageBand is whether or not the instrument uses a generator to make sound.

If you are feeling brave, you can adjust the settings inside the Track Info window for the current instrument and then close the Track Info window, and your changes will be applied to the instrument and be saved along with your current song when you save your song.

However, if you change the track's instrument before saving your song, your changes will be lost.

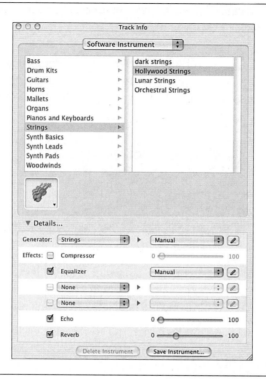

FIGURE 3.11
Secrets of the Track Info window: the expanded version or Behind the Scenes of Hollywood Strings.

SAVING AN INSTRUMENT

If you tweak the settings in your current instrument and then attempt to change the instrument for the current track, you will get a dialog asking you if you want to save the file before switching to a new one. You can select Don't Save, which simply forgets the tweaks that you made and loads the new instrument. If you select Save, you are presented with a Save As dialog, which allows you to save your tweaked instrument under a name of your own invention.

You can also click the Save Instrument button in the lower-right corner of the Track Info window and you will be presented with the same Save As dialog.

Again, we will go much more into depth with creating your own Software Instruments in Chapter 8.

tip
You can download this project file and a MP3 of the completed song from `http://macaudioguy.com/gbb/downloads/`.

CREATING A JAZZ TUNE

Tired of just playing a few notes? Want to jam a little? Good. Let's put together a jazz tune using some Software Instruments.

WE GOT RHYTHM

First, let's launch GarageBand and create a new song:

1. Select File ····➔ New. Keep the tempo at 120bpm and set the key to A using the Key menu. Finally, let's name the song **Jazz Thang** and click Create.

2. Get rid of the Grand Piano track for now. Select Track ····➔ Delete Track (or press ⌘-Delete).

3 To create a Real Instrument track for your drums (in order to save processor power), select Track ····> New Track (or press Shift-⌘-N).

4 In the New Track window, click Real Instrument and then click Drums and Detailed Drums. Then click OK to create the track for our drums.

5 Next, open the Loop Browser by clicking the Loop Browser button (or press ⌘-L). Expand the Loop Browser by dragging the Control Bar up. Select Drums and Jazz from the Loop Browser.

6 Drag the Lounge Jazz Drums 01 loop to the timeline. Drag the right side of the region (using the curved-arrow cursor) to extend the loop to the right. Drag it all the way to the other side of the screen and let the timeline scroll automatically to the right. Extend it to 32 measures, stopping at the start of measure 33.

7 Go back to the Loop Browser and click Drums to deselect the Drums button while still keeping Jazz selected.

8 Next, click Bass and drag the Cool Upright Bass 01 loop to measure 1 of the timeline just below our drum track.

9 Drag the right side of the region (again, using the curved-arrow cursor) to extend the loop to the right. Drag it all the way to the other side of the screen and let the timeline scroll automatically to the right. Extend it to 32 measures, stopping at the start of measure 33. One more track and we'll have a groove.

10 Go back to the Loop Browser and click Bass to deselect the Bass button while keeping Jazz selected. Click Elec. Piano and drag the Fusion Electric Piano 12 loop to measure 1 of the timeline just below our bass track.

11 Drag the right side of the region (using the curved-arrow cursor) to extend the loop to the right. Drag it all the way to the other side of the screen and let the timeline scroll automatically to the right. Extend it to 32 measures, stopping at the start of measure 33.

12 Finally, click Cycle to turn on the Cycle Section and drag the Cycle Section bar so that it covers from the beginning of measure 1 to the beginning of measure 33. Click Play to hear your rather sleepy jazz rhythm section.

SOLO TIME

Now that we've got our rhythm section groovin', let's lay a solo on top.

1 Go to the Track menu and select New Track (or press Shift-⌘-N). In the New Track window, click Software Instrument. Next, select Woodwinds and then Alto Sax. Click OK.

2 While this is an okay-sounding sax, let's bump it to the next level. Open the Track Info window for the sax track. Click the Details triangle. Next, let's tweak the reverb effect up to about 75% and the echo effect up to about 50%, as shown in Figure 3.12.

> **tip**
>
> All Software Instrument loops become Real Instrument loops when dragged to a Real Instrument track. This is a very important concept for getting more tracks out of GarageBand. Real Instrument tracks barely impact your Mac's processor compared to the heavy toll that Software Instrument tracks demand.

FIGURE 3.12
A little reverb and a little echo and we have an alto sax suitable for a rainy night solo.

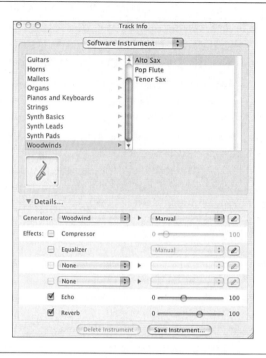

3 Close the Track Info window by clicking the red button in the upper-left corner of the window.

You should now have a very wet and lonely sounding alto sax with which to play your solo. What about your solo? That's up to you. Hit the Record button and let's see what you got, baby!

Be sure to save this song for future reference, and so that all your hard work isn't lost.

RECORDING YOUR GUITAR

I t is probably safe to say that most musicians in the United States play guitar. Apple realized that for GarageBand to succeed, it needed to be guitar friendly. After all, a garage band with a bunch of keyboardists just doesn't say rock 'n' roll.

In the previous two chapters we showed you how to record backing tracks using Apple Loops and a keyboard. Now we'll show you how to use GarageBand's Real Instrument recording capabilities to lay down some guitar tracks.

GETTING YOUR GUITAR TO PLAY WELL WITH GARAGEBAND

Plugging your guitar into your Mac might seem unnatural, but it's actually no more difficult than plugging it into your amp. In this section we'll show you some do's and don'ts on getting your guitar, your Mac, and Garageband set up to record your guitar.

It's a good idea to take a look at Appendix B, "Configuring Your Studio," to get the lowdown on all the ways you can physically hook up your guitar to your Mac before we get started.

SETTING AUDIO LEVELS

The most critical and most often overlooked aspect of getting a great recorded guitar sound is properly setting up the audio input levels. There is nothing nice about digital clipping distortion from recording too hot, and once it's recorded you can't "fix it in the mix."

GUITAR VOLUME

The first link in this chain is the volume control on your guitar. A lot of guitarists start with their volume knob set at 5. Then, after the recording engineer has carefully set the input levels for the recorder, the guitarist will decide that they need more volume and turn their guitar volume up.

Don't do this. Set you guitar volume at 10 and leave it alone—unless your guitar does the snap, crackle, and pop when it's set to 10; then you can turn it down a little. Later in this chapter we'll show you how to set up monitoring so you can hear yourself clearly.

KEEP IT SIMPLE

Use your best guitar cord and, depending on your configuration, plug it directly into the preamp, mixer, or Mac (following). Using high-quality cables with as few connectors as possible is the best way to keep an infuriating pop or buzz from ruining your otherwise stellar performance. If you are using a preamp or a mixer, make sure that your volume levels are set properly and are not distorted. If you're not sure how to set your audio levels, take a look at the section on setting levels in Chapter 5, "Recording Vocals and Other Instruments."

AVOID USING STOMP BOXES

Most guitar players use outboard guitar effects, often called *stomp boxes*, to shape their guitar sound.

Do yourself a favor. Avoid using stomp boxes.

GarageBand's high-quality effects and guitar amp simulations usually allow you to get the guitar sound you are looking for without using stomp boxes.

These effects are problematic for recording. Usually these boxes use relatively low-quality electronics and can be noisy. Making sure that the connections between effects are noise free and that the volumes are set properly can be a nightmare. Remember that a signal chain can only sound as good as its weakest link.

CONFIGURING YOUR MAC'S SOUND INPUT SETTINGS

If your guitar is hooked up to your Mac audio-in port, rather than through an external audio interface, you'll need to set input levels in the Sound pane of your Mac's System Preferences.

To set your Mac's sound input levels:

1 Select the Apple menu, and select System Preferences.

2 Select Sound.

3 Click Input.

4 Select your sound input device from the sound input menu.

In most cases your sound input device is Line In, as shown in Figure 4.1. However, depending on your Mac model it might be External Microphone/Line In or Sound Input.

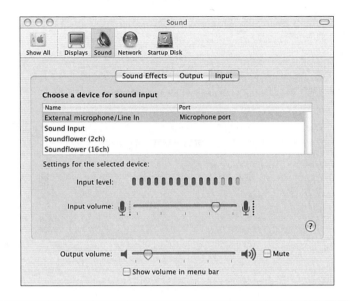

FIGURE 4.1
The Sound pane of the System Preferences menu is where you control input volume levels.

Next, you need to play your guitar at a typical volume level. Set the input volume to your Mac using the Input volume slider. You want to set the volume level so that when you're playing your loudest, the second segment from the right of the Input level meter is illuminated as shown in Figure 4.1.

SETTING THE INPUT VOLUME OF AN EXTERNAL AUDIO INTERFACE

If you are using an audio interface to get sound into your Mac, you need to consult the device's documentation on how to set input levels. For example, Griffin Technology's iMic uses your Mac's Speech Recognition pane to set input levels. Go figure.

SETTING GARAGEBAND'S AUDIO PREFERENCES

Now that you have sound coming into your Mac, you need to set GarageBand's Audio Preferences (see Figure 4.2):

1 Launch GarageBand.

2 Select GarageBand ⋯⟩ Preferences.

3 Next select the Audio/MIDI tab in the Preferences panel.

4 Set the Audio Input and Output menus to the name of your audio device.

If you're hooked into your Mac's Audio-in port, select Built-in Audio. If you are using an audio interface, select its name from the drop-down menu. If your audio interface's name does not appear, check to ensure that you installed any drivers that may have come with your device.

Next, set the Optimize for radio button to Minimum delay when playing instruments live. This is to minimize latency when recording. Refer to Chapter 5.

tip
To be safe, you should set the Input level every time you hook up your guitar.

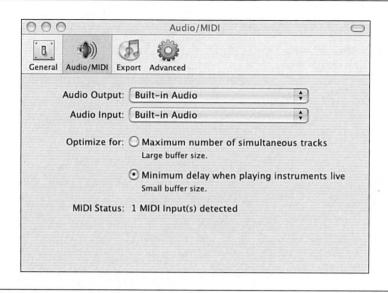

FIGURE 4.2
The Audio/MIDI pane of GarageBand's Preferences panel is yet another bus stop on the path to GarageBand audio nirvana.

CHOOSING AN AMPLIFIER

Now is when the fun starts. One of the super-cool features of GarageBand is its selection of tasty guitar Real Instruments, which include amp simulations coupled with some really cool effects. One of our friends calls it "Beck in a box." (Jeff Beck, not just Beck, silly.)

Finally, you can record your guitar directly and have it sound like you are playing through an amp. Your Mac masquerading as a Marshall stack, who would've thunk?

PLAYING A GUITAR REAL INSTRUMENT PRESET

Go ahead and launch GarageBand if you haven't already done so, and follow these steps to set up a new project:

1 Create a new song by selecting File ⋯⟩ New (or pressing ⌘-N).

2 Name your song **Amp test** and click Create.

3 Get rid of the pesky Grand Piano track by selecting Track ⋯⟩ Delete Track (or pressing ⌘-Delete).

4 Create a new track by selecting Track ⋯⟩ New Track (or pressing Option-⌘-N).

5 In the New Track window, click Real Instrument and then select Guitars in the left pane. In the right pane select Classic Rock.

6 Set Format to Stereo and Monitor to On, as shown in Figure 4.3, and then click OK.

FIGURE 4.3
Whether you want your guitar to sound like U2 or Eric Clapton, there's a Guitar preset for you in the New Track window.

You should be able to play your guitar now and have it sound like you are playing through an amp with a basic classic rock sound. Can you say Deep Purple?

To try out some different amp sounds, select Track ····} Show Track Info (or press Option-⌘-I). In the Track Info window, choose one of the other guitar Real Instrument effects, like Arena Rock, and then close the Track Info window. Go ahead and repeat this process to try out other Guitar presets.

MODIFYING REAL INSTRUMENT SETTINGS

GarageBand's preset Real Instrument effects are cool and useful, but how about creating your own sound? Let's dig a little deeper into the magic of GarageBand's Real Instrument effects. Open the Track Info window by selecting Track ····} Show Track Info. In the Track Info window, click the triangle labeled Details in the lower-left corner of the window (see Figure 4.4).

If you are feeling brave, you can click the button with the pencil icon on the far right of the Amp Simulation row and bring up the Amp Simulation settings window shown in Figure 4.5.

note

If you make any tweaks to the settings during your experimentation, you might be presented with a Save dialog. Don't panic. Simply select Don't Save if you want to discard your changes and switch to another guitar. For more information on saving the new settings, see "Saving Real Instrument Settings" just a little further on in this chapter.

FIGURE 4.4
The Details tab in the Track Info window reveals all the gory details behind a Guitar preset.

FIGURE 4.5
The Amp Simulation settings window is chock full of ways to adjust the way your amp sounds.

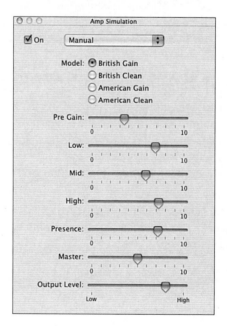

There are buttons to push and sliders to slide. Tweak away, my friend.

When you've got something you like, close the Amp Simulation settings window and the Track Info window and your changes will be applied to the instrument and will be saved along with your current song.

SAVING REAL INSTRUMENT SETTINGS

If you tweak the settings in your current instrument and then attempt to change the instrument for the current track, you will get a dialog asking you if you want to save the file before switching to a new one. You can select Don't Save, which simply forgets the tweaks that you made and loads the new instrument. If you select Save, you are presented with a Save As dialog which will allow you to save your tweaked instrument under a name of your own invention.

You can also click Save Instrument in the lower-right corner of the Track Info window and you will be presented with the same Save As dialog that allows you to save your tweaked instrument under a name of your own invention.

> **note**
>
> We will go much more into depth with creating your own Software and Real Instruments in Chapter 8, "Making Your Own Software and Real Instruments."

RECORDING YOUR PERFORMANCE

Time to get down to recording some tracks. Now that you've got your guitar hooked up and you've tried a couple of GarageBand's guitar Real Instrument settings, let's record.

RECORDING A BASIC GUITAR TRACK

If you are happy with the Track settings from the previous section, go ahead and use those settings.

Otherwise, click Track Info and then select Guitars and Classic Rock. Next, set Format to Stereo and Monitor to On, as shown previously in Figure 4.3. Then close the window to accept these basic settings.

To record a track

1 Play your guitar just to make sure you've still got audio happening.

2 To use a metronome while recording, select Control ⸱⸱⸱⟩ Metronome.

3 To hear a one-measure count-in before recording, select Control ⸱⸱⸱⟩ Count In.

4 Move the playhead to where you want to begin recording.

5 Click the Record button (R) to begin recording.

tip

Record only a portion of a song—in other words, a verse, a chorus, or a solo—with each recording pass. This will give you much more flexibility in editing regions and tracks.

note

We'll cover region editing in depth in the "Region Editing Using the Track Editor" section of Chapter 6, "Editing and Mixing Your Music." In Chapter 9, "Making Your Own Loops," we'll show you techniques to turn your Real Instrument tracks into Real Instrument loops for even more editing flexibility.

6 Play something with your guitar.

7 Click Play or press the spacebar to turn recording off and to pause playback.

8 Click Go to Beginning to return to the start of the song.

9 Click Play to play back what you just recorded.

Notice that you created a region when you recorded. You can manipulate the region you just created like any other region. See "Moving Regions" in Chapter 2, "Making Music with Apple Loops."

If you are unhappy with your recording, you can erase the track by selecting the region(s) in the track's timeline and pressing the Delete key. To only replace a portion of your recording, check out the next two main sections of this chapter, "Editing Your Performance" and "Overdubbing Your Guitar."

EDITING YOUR PERFORMANCE

One of the cool things about GarageBand is that you don't have to be a perfect guitar player to get a near-perfect recording. All it takes is a little editing.

USING THE REAL INSTRUMENT TRACK EDITOR

When you recorded your guitar, you created what GarageBand calls a Real Instrument *track*. You'll notice that the track regions are a purple color as opposed to the blue and green regions we worked with in the previous chapters.

The Real Instrument track is slightly different from the previously discussed tracks in that your track editing options are rather limited. In fact, in the Track Editing window the only thing you can edit is the selected region's name.

You can, however, perform all of the same region manipulations to the track in the Track Editor that you can perform in the timeline. These include splitting and joining regions as well as the usual edit functions of cutting, copying, and pasting. Editing by manipulating regions is discussed in depth in Chapter 2.

A TRACK OF A DIFFERENT COLOR

You may have noticed that, in GarageBand, the regions in the timeline seem to come in a variety of pleasing pastel shades.

These pastels are actually a color code for the various types of tracks (see Figure 4.6).

FIGURE 4.6
While the different track types appear as shades of gray in this figure, they are actually soothing shades of blue, green, and purple.

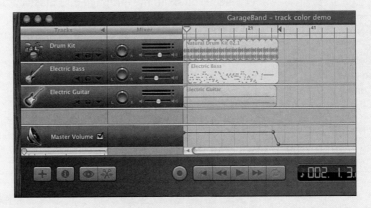

- **Light blue**—These regions are Real Instrument Apple Loops, which are discussed in Chapter 2.
- **Light green**—These regions are either Software Instrument Apple Loops, which are discussed in Chapter 2, or Software Instrument tracks, which are discussed in Chapter 3, "Recording Your Own Music with Software Instruments."
- **Light purple**—These regions are Real Instrument tracks, which are discussed in this chapter and Chapter 5.

If you happen to be color-blind, take heart in the fact that you can always refer to the Track Info window to identify a track's type.

OVERDUBBING YOUR GUITAR

Overdubbing is a recording technique to combine the best parts of several performances or takes into one mistake-free track. Overdubbing is the safest method to fix any mistakes in your performance.

THE DOUBLE-DOG SUPER-SAFE OVERDUB METHOD

To make absolutely sure that none of your original performance is lost while still being able fix a bad note or phrase, use this technique.

Let's pretend that you just laid down a killer track using the Classic Rock Real Instrument, except for that little boo-boo on measure 9.

> **note**
> The only downside to the "double-dog super-safe" method is that you're going to create two or more tracks with the associated load on your system. Use as few Software Instrument tracks as possible to get more Real Instrument tracks.

CLONING THE TRACK

First we'll duplicate, or *clone*, the track:

1 Select Track ⋯⟩ New Track.

2 Select Guitars in the left page and Classic Rock in the right pane of the New Track window.

3 Click OK to create the new track.

4 Select your killer track and select Edit ⋯⟩ Copy.

5 Select the new track and select Edit ⋯⟩ Paste.

See Figure 4.7 for the results of this operation.

tip

Or you could have just Option-dragged your killer track to the new track instead of doing steps 4 and 5.

FIGURE 4.7
Cloning your killer track provides a safety net for further evil experiments.

REMOVING MISTAKES

Note that GarageBand conveniently named the new cloned track `killer track. 1 for us`.

Next, we want to get rid of measure 9 in the cloned track:

1 Move the playhead so that it is aligned with the beginning of measure 9.

2 Select Edit ⋯⟩ Split (or press ⌘-T).

3 Move the playhead to the beginning of measure 10.

4 Again select Edit ⋯⟩ Split.

5 Select the region that you have just created on measure 9.

6 Select Edit ····} Delete; see Figure 4.8.

FIGURE 4.8
After cloning our killer track, we surgically removed the offending measure 9.

RECORDING YOUR OVERDUB

To be triple safe, we are going to record on yet another track to replace measure 9:

1 Mute the original killer track.

2 Select Track ····} New Track and then select Guitars and then Classic Rock in the New Track window.

3 Click OK to create the track.

4 Click Go to Beginning to move the playhead to the start of the song.

5 Click Record.

6 Start playing along with the cloned track a couple measures before measure 9 and play a measure or two beyond measure 9.

7 Click Play to turn off recording and to pause playback.

8 Click Go to Beginning.

9 Click Play to hear what you just recorded.

If you're happy with the new measure 9, you can resize the region to only show measure 9 (see Figure 4.9).

FIGURE 4.9
The new and improved and trimmed-to-fit measure 9 is ready for its audition with the rest of the killer track.

CLEANING UP

You could leave your tracks sprawled out like this. But for neatness sake, you really should clean up a little.

To clean up this mess, do the following:

1. Move the new measure 9 region into the hole you created in the previous track by dragging the region into the blank measure 9.

2. Then, if you are feeling really bold, go ahead and delete your original killer track.

3. Finally, select the two now-empty tracks and select Track ⸱⸱⸱⸱⸢ Delete Track for each.

THE FILL-IN-THE-BLANK CYCLE REGION OVERDUB METHOD

The advantage to this type of overdub, sometimes called a *punch-in*, is that it is quick and you don't have to create a bunch of extra tracks. You don't have to do any of the copy/paste stuff that you did in the previous method; you just record and you're done.

The disadvantage is that there is the potential for lost data. You can minimize this risk by working on a cloned track as described in the previous section.

SETTING UP A CYCLE REGION

Let's pretend that you discover a slight bobble at measure 17 of your previously recorded killer track.

Turn on the cycle region by clicking Cycle. Drag the cycle region so that it's over measure 17 on the beat ruler, as shown in Figure 4.10.

FIGURE 4.10
We are targeting measure 17 for annihilation by using the yellow cycle region bar.

The Cycle Region Bar

RECORDING YOUR OVERDUB

Select Control ⋯▷ Count In to give yourself a one-measure count-in before recording; otherwise, recording will start immediately upon clicking Record. Yikes!

1 Get ready to play your guitar.

2 Click Record.

3 Start playing your guitar.

4 Notice that GarageBand automatically starts recording at the start of the cycle region, stops recording at the end of the cycle region, and starts cycling in Play mode.

5 Click Play to pause playback. Notice that you have a new region with your newly recorded overdub on measure 17.

If the overdub sucked, select Edit ⋯▷ Undo (or press ⌘-Z) to try again. Otherwise, call it a done dub.

tip

If you clone the track that you wish to over-dub, you can set up a larger cycle region than just the region you wish to replace. Then you can resize the region to only use the portion that you wish to replace.

tip

You can download this project file and a MP3 of the completed song from `http://macaudioguy.com/gbb/downloads/`.

RECORDING A ROCK SONG

Let's use what you've learned in the last few chapters to create a rock-n-roll tune. GarageBand is going to supply the drums, bass, and rhythm guitar for this song. All you have to do is work on your lead guitar part and your British accent.

Let's rock!

FEEL THE RHYTHM

We'll use some Apple Loops to put together a rhythm section. Tell your drummer to chill until the next chapter. If your bass player is really itching to play, have them double the part that we'll lay down. And then, when they're not looking, lose their track.

Okay, you know the drill:

1　Launch GarageBand.

2　Select File ⤑ New to create a new song.

3　Name this one **Guitaro** and set it to the key of A.

4　Click Create.

5　Select the Grand Piano track.

6　Select Track ⤑ Delete Track to dump the piano.

DRUMS, DUDE

We'll lay in a quick-and-dirty drum loop. You can experiment with some different beats later:

1　Click Loop Browser to open the Loop Browser.

2　Select the Drums and the Rock/Blues buttons.

3　Scroll down in the Loop Browser to find `Live Edgy Drums 11`.

4　Drag `Live Edgy Drums 11` to the first track of the timeline.

5　Drag the region so that it starts on measure 5.

6　Drag the right side of the region using the curved-arrow cursor to extend the loop to the right.

7 Extend the loop to the beginning of measure 41.

8 Drag the Zoom slider to fit the entire track in the timeline window.

The result should look like Figure 4.11.

FIGURE 4.11
Like oaks from acorns, rock songs start with a drum track.

BASS FISHIN'

Let's go fish for a bass line in the Loop Browser:

1 Click Drums in the Loop Browser to deactivate it.

2 Click Bass.

3 Scroll down in the Loop Browser to find `Alternative Rock Bass 01`.

4 Drag `Alternative Rock Bass 01` to below the drum track on the timeline.

5 Drag the region so that it starts on measure 1.

6 Drag the right side of the region using the curved-arrow cursor to extend the loop to the right.

7 Extend the loop to the beginning of measure 13.

Now, let's add a second bass loop to add interest to the song:

1 Scroll down in the Loop Browser to find `Alternative Rock Bass 02`.

2 Drag `Alternative Rock Bass 02` to measure 13 behind the `Alternative Rock Bass 01` region on the timeline.

3 Select the `Alternative Rock Bass 01` region.

4 Copy (or Option-drag) the `Alternative Rock Bass 01` region to measure 17 behind the `Alternative Rock Bass 02` region on the timeline.

5 Drag the right side of the region using the curved-arrow cursor to scale down the loop so that it ends at the beginning of measure 25.

6 Select the `Alternative Rock Bass 02` region.

7 Copy the `Alternative Rock Bass 02` region to measure 25 behind the `Alternative Rock Bass 01` region on the timeline.

8 Shift-select the last `Alternative Rock Bass 01` region and the last `Alternative Rock Bass 02` region.

9 Copy the selected `Alternative Rock Bass 01` region and the `Alternative Rock Bass 02` region to measure 29 behind the `Alternative Rock Bass 02` region on the timeline.

10 Select the last `Alternative Rock Bass 02` region.

11 Drag the right side of the region using the curved-arrow cursor to resize the region so that it ends at the beginning of measure 45.

Who said playing bass was easy? Actually, the reason we made such a seemingly complex bass line is that we are starting to build a verse and chorus structure to the song.

You should now have something that looks like Figure 4.12.

FIGURE 4.12
The bass line is the skeleton of a rock song, but don't tell the bass player that.

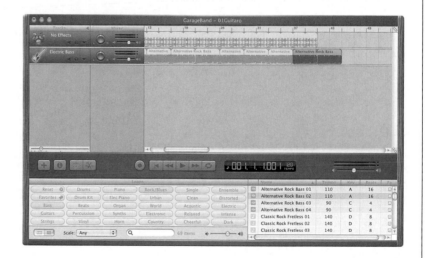

RHYTHM GUITAR A LA U2

We're going to lay down a killer rhythm guitar track with some cool chord changes to give you something to work with when you lay down your lead track.

The bass track we just recorded has a chord progression that goes A, G, F#, G, A for the verse parts and does an A, C, A, G, D thing in the chorus section. We'll use GarageBand's transpose feature to keep the rhythm guitar in key with the bass. If this is all Greek to you, don't worry about it. You'll get it by ear.

Go back to the Loop Browser and do the following:

1 Click Bass in the Loop Browser to deactivate it.

2 Click Guitars.

3 Scroll down in the Loop Browser to find the Echoing String 02 loop.

4 Drag the Echoing String 02 loop to below the bass track on the timeline.

5 Drag the region so that it starts on measure 5.

6 Copy (or Option-drag) the Echoing String 02 loop region to measure 6 behind the first Echoing String 02 region on the timeline.

7 Repeat copying the Echoing String 02 loop region to measures 7 and 8.

You should now have four copies of the Echoing String 02 loop between measures 5 and 9. Now we're going to do some transposing to make these loops follow the bass line:

1 Select the Echoing String 02 loop region on measure 6.

2 Click Track Edit, which brings up the Track Edit window in place of the Loop Browser window.

3 Drag the Transpose slider to the left until the Transpose window indicates −2.

4 Select the Echoing String 02 loop region on measure 7.

5 Drag the Transpose slider in the Track Edit window to the left until the Transpose window indicates −3.

6 Select the Echoing String 02 loop region on measure 8.

7 Drag the Transpose slider in the Track Edit window to the left until the Transpose window indicates −2.

8 Select all four loop regions of Echoing String 02.

9 Copy (or Option-drag) all four loop regions of Echoing String 02 to measure 9 behind the first four Echoing String 02 regions on the timeline.

10 Click Play to hear what you have so far.

11 Click Play again to pause playback.

12 Click Go to Beginning to go to the start of the song.

Now we have a very cool little verse section to the song. Let's drop in a chorus, shall we:

1 Click Browser to bring up the Loop Browser.

2 Select the Guitars and Rock/Blues buttons.

3 Scroll down in the Loop Browser to find Echoing String 01.

4 Drag the Echoing String 01 loop to measure 13 behind our other rhythm guitar regions on the timeline.

5 Drag the right side of the region using the curved-arrow cursor to resize the region so that it ends at the beginning of measure 17.

6 Select all the loop regions of the rhythm guitar track.

7 Copy (or Option-drag) all the regions of the rhythm guitar track to measure 17 behind the first rhythm guitar region on the timeline.

8 Select all the loop regions of the rhythm guitar track that you just copied.

9 Copy all the regions that you just copied to measure 29 on the timeline.

10 Select the last Echoing String 01 loop region.

11 Drag the right side of the region using the curved-arrow cursor to resize the region so that it ends at the beginning of measure 45.

Check out Figure 4.13 to see how our rhythm guitar track should look.

Now we've got this really awesome rhythm groove going; all it needs is a few hot licks from your guitar to make it a chart topper.

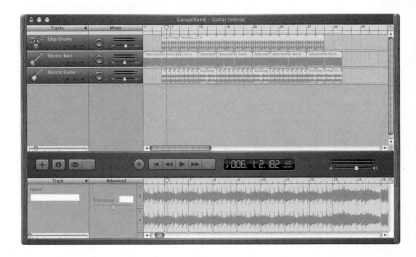

FIGURE 4.13
It took a lot of region manipulation, but the results rock. All we need now is a lead guitar part.

LAYING DOWN THE LEAD

Your approach to the recording of your lead part depends on how powerful your Mac is. There is no real way to know how many tracks you have left. It's like getting a speeding ticket when you don't have a speedometer.

If, when you add more tracks, your Mac starts to choke and give you errors, you can still put together a lead part as long as you have one Real Instrument track left to work with. However, the more tracks that you have left, the more flexible your recording technique can be.

We'll presume that you still have at least two tracks left to record your guitar part. We'll lay down the song's verse parts on one track and the choruses and solo on a second track.

Still have your guitar hooked up? If not, get it hooked up and get ready to play.

To record the verse track using cycle recording

1 Select Track ┈┤ New Track.

2 Select Real Instrument.

3 Select Guitars in the left pane and Dreamy Shimmer in the right pane.

4 In the Format row, select the Stereo radio button.

5 In the Monitor row, select the On radio button.

> **tip**
> One way to gain more tracks is to set all of your previous tracks to No Effects using the Track Info window. But if you have at least a 733MHz G4, you should be able to get at least six Real Instrument tracks, even with effects.

tips

An easy way to tune your guitar before starting a new track is to use a Software Instrument and record an E, A, D, G, B, E sequence. Then use this song as a reference to tune your guitar.

You can play back your backing tracks at a slower tempo to practice before you record, and your Software Instrument and Real Instrument parts will remain in tune. But be sure to set the tempo back to where you want it for the song before recording your guitar part.

6 Click OK to close the New Track window.

7 Click Cycle.

8 Drag the cycle region to cover from the start of measure 5 to the start of measure 13.

9 Select Control ⤍ Metronome if you want to hear a metronome.

10 Select Control ⤍ Count In if you want to hear a one-measure count-in before recording.

11 Click Record to begin recording.

12 Play your guitar.

13 Recording will automatically stop at the end of measure 12 and playback of the cycle region will begin.

14 Click Play to pause playback.

Decide if you would like to keep the take. If you would like to re-record the part, click Go to Beginning to go to the start of the song and then repeat the cycle recording process until you get something that you like.

To record the second verse, drag the cycle region to cover from the start of measure 17 to the start of measure 25. Then repeat the cycle record process. Or you can copy the region you recorded for the first verse to the second verse. The second verse of this song is between measures 17 and 25.

We'll create a new track to record the chorus and solo guitar parts for our song:

1 Select Track ⤍ New Track.

2 Select Real Instrument.

3 Select Guitars in the left pane and Arena Rock in the right pane.

4 In the Format row, select the Stereo radio button.

5 In the Monitor row, select the On radio button.

6 Click OK to close the New Track window.

7 Click Cycle.

8 Drag the cycle region to cover from the start of measure 13 to the start of measure 17.

9   Select Control ⋯⫸ Metronome if you want to hear a metronome.

10   Select Control ⋯⫸ Count In if you want to hear a one-measure count-in before recording.

11   Click Record to begin recording.

12   Play your guitar.

13   Recording automatically stops at the end of measure 17 and playback of the cycle region begins.

14   Click Play to pause playback.

Decide if you would like to keep the take. If you would like to re-record the part, repeat the cycle recording process until you get something that you like.

Copy the region you recorded for the first chorus to the second chorus of the song. The second chorus of this song is between measures 25 and 29. Also copy the chorus region to measure 37 and then extend the region to the start of measure 45 using the loop cursor. This will be the chorus repeat to close to our song.

Finally, we'll record the solo part on the same track that we recorded the choruses and drag the cycle region to cover from the start of measure 25 to the start of measure 37. Repeat the cycle recording process until you have a solo that's going to bring down the house.

Add a quick fade-out to the end of the song by selecting Track ⋯⫸ Show Master Track. On the master track, click the Master Volume check box. Next, create a control point by clicking the master track volume curve at measure 41. Create another control point at measure 45 and drag the point to the bottom of the track timeline (see the Master Track in Figure 4.14).

Our completed rock song should look like Figure 4.14, except that your guitar parts will be a lot cooler than ours. Be sure to save this song for future reference, and so that all your hard work isn't lost.

FIGURE 4.14
It's only a rock-n-roll song, but we like it!

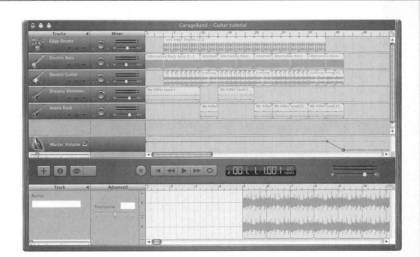

Now we have one frigging awesome rock tune; all it needs is some lyrics. Or not. In the next chapter, we'll pull out the microphones and show you how to record vocals and other live instruments.

RECORDING VOCALS AND OTHER INSTRUMENTS

5

GarageBand's ability to record audio is probably its most powerful feature. You can record your vocals with a mic and a couple of adaptors directly into GarageBand. Add an audio interface or a mixer and the recording possibilities are endless. With a microphone or two and GarageBand, you can record your vocals, your didgeridoo stylings, or even your unique hubcap drum kit.

Let's take a look at how to use GarageBand's Real Instrument recording capabilities to record your singing or just about anything else that makes noise.

USING MICROPHONES AND HEADPHONES

If you are a singer or play a musical instrument other than keyboards or guitar, you'll need to use a mic to get your sound into GarageBand.

CONNECTING MICROPHONES

You can use a single vocal mic hooked directly into your Mac to record your voice. But using a mic preamp and an audio interface will give you higher-quality results and more flexibility.

If you are using a stereo pair of mics to record an instrument, a stereo audio interface built preamp is the way to go.

If you want to use three or more mics to record your entire band, you will need a mixer or, better yet, a mixer with an audio interface.

BASIC MICROPHONE TECHNIQUES

Recording engineers spend lifetimes perfecting microphone techniques. We'll show you a couple tried-and-true techniques to improve the quality of your recordings.

note

If you don't already own a microphone, or to learn more about all the ways you can connect microphones to your Mac, take a look at Appendix B, "Configuring Your Studio."

**caution**

Audio feedback can cause hearing damage. Turn off speakers when recording with mics.

Whether you choose a dynamic or condenser mic (see the sidebar "Choosing a Microphone" in Appendix B), there are a couple things you can do to improve recording quality when you record vocals:

- **Use a mic stand**—Handholding a mic on stage is a great way to show off your moves to your adoring fans, but save it for the stage. Using a mic stand while recording avoids handling noise and allows you to sing at the proper distance from the mic.

- **Don't eat the mic**—The proper distance is with your mouth 8''–12'' from the mic.

- **Sing slightly off-axis**—Position yourself about 15° off from singing directly into the mic. This will cut down on annoying pops.

Microphone techniques can vary wildly depending on what you are recording; vocals, guitar amps, sousaphones, kazoos, and so on all demand their own approach. We suggest that you pick up a book on the subject and experiment to find which techniques work best for your instrument.

USING HEADPHONES

Any time you are recording with a microphone and you have speakers connected, you have the potential for audio feedback, that ear-piercing screech that we all know and hate.

The way around this problem is to make sure that speakers are turned off when recording with mics. Use headphones to listen with while you're recording. This is called *monitoring*.

INPUT MONITORING IN GARAGEBAND

When you create a new Real Instrument track in GarageBand, there is a monitor radio button, which is set by default to Off, as shown in Figure 5.1. Monitoring is set this way to avoid feedback problems.

FIGURE 5.1
The Monitor option is set to Off for your protection.

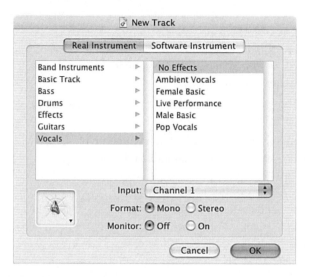

After you have created a Real Instrument track, you can turn on monitoring to hear yourself by clicking Track Info and setting the Monitor radio button to On. Just make sure that your speakers are off and your headphones are on.

MINIMIZING LATENCY

No, latency is not when you show up to rehearsal a half an hour late without any beer—that's just called rude, dude.

Latency is the delay between when you sing into the mic and when you hear yourself in the headphones. This is the time that it takes your Mac or audio interface to process audio into GarageBand. This delay can range from barely perceptible to bloody annoying. To minimize this delay in GarageBand, select GarageBand ⋯⋗ Preferences. Then select the Audio/MIDI tab. Set the Optimize radio button to Minimum delay when playing instruments live (see Figure 5.2).

If you are using an external audio interface, it may have software or hardware settings to minimize latency. Consult your documentation.

tips

A good practice is to turn Monitoring to Off except when you are rehearsing or recording a part.

Reducing latency by selecting Minimum delay negatively affects your computer's performance. After recording, set the Optimize radio button back to Maximum number of simultaneous tracks.

FIGURE 5.2
Sometimes a smaller buffer size is better.

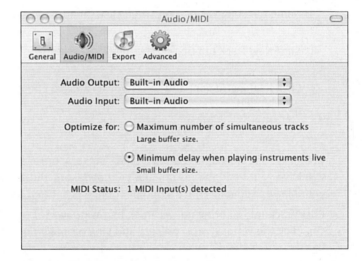

SETTING GARAGEBAND'S INPUT LEVELS

Nothing is more critical to the quality of your recording as setting proper audio recording levels. Repeat this phrase in your head until it becomes your mantra.

Setting up your Mac's audio input levels as well as setting the input levels and Audio preferences in GarageBand are pretty much the same for microphones as for guitars. You can refer to the sections "Configuring Your Mac's Sound Input Settings," "Setting the Input Volume of an External Audio Interface," and "Setting GarageBand's Audio Preferences" in Chapter 4, "Recording Your Guitar" to review how we set up levels for guitar. Also take a look at Appendix B's section "Hooking a Microphone Directly to Your Mac."

The most important thing to remember in setting your input levels for GarageBand is to not allow GarageBand's level meters to go into the red zone. If the red dots next to the level meters light while you are recording, turn down the input level slider by dragging it slightly to the left; then try your recording again.

SETTING UP YOUR VOCAL STYLE

As any Saturday night karaoke singer will tell you, a little reverb can help just about any voice. GarageBand takes this even further with a bunch of vocal effect presets designed by professional engineers that combine not only reverb, but also effects like equalizers, compressors, and delays. These allow you to benefit from the same "subtle" vocal enhancement that Justin and Britney enjoy.

EFFECTS 101

Just like the guitar effects we discussed in the previous chapter, GarageBand's vocal effect presets are called *Real Instrument presets*.

Let's browse some of the Real Instrument presets that Apple has provided to see how they affect your vocal sound:

1 Launch GarageBand and create a new song by selecting File ···⟩ New.

2 Name the song `Vocal Test`. Then click Create.

3 Click New Track to bring up the New Track window.

4 Click Real Instrument and select Vocals and No Effects for now.

5 Click OK to create a new track.

Before we audition GarageBand's effect presets, make sure your mic is hooked up, you have your headphones on, and your speakers and amplifiers are off. And that your Mac or audio interface's output volume is set to a reasonable level.

Click Track Info to bring up the Track Info window. Set the Monitor radio button to On. Click the various vocal presets and sing or make noise to hear what they sound like.

You may find a favorite preset and use it for all of your recordings, or you might like to try different effects for different songs or parts of songs.

Don't limit yourself to just the vocal presets. Take a few minutes and go through all of the Real Instrument presets. You may find that the Drums, Crunchy Drums preset is just what you need to get that Trent Reznor sound that you've been looking for.

Once you've found a preset that you like, go ahead and close the Track Info window.

CHANGING EFFECTS AFTER RECORDING

As an experiment, let's record a short vocal track. We'll presume that you have everything from the previous section set up:

1 Click Cycle. You should see a yellow cycle region bar above measures 1–4.

2 Click Record and then sing or make some noise.

3 Recording stops at the end of measure 4, and the track begins to cycle playback of the recording. Let the playback continue to cycle.

4 Click Track Info to bring up the Track Info window, and set the Monitor radio button to Off, as shown in Figure 5.3.

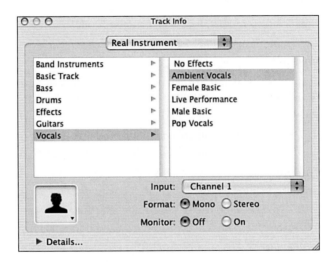

FIGURE 5.3
The good old Track Info window, showing its fine selection of vocal Real Instrument presets.

5 While your recording is playing back, try different Real Instrument presets.

6 After trying the effects, select Vocals ⸱⸱⸱⸱▸ No effects. And then close the Track Info window.

7 Click Play to pause playback.

We want you to notice one big thing from this little experiment: Effects are not recorded.

Your voice was recorded into GarageBand with no effects applied to it. The effects are applied to the track as it plays back. This means that you can go back to any track at any time and change its effect settings.

This is a very important concept. It gives you the ultimate flexibility in trying different effects to see which effect suits the particular track. It also means that the more effects you add, the harder your Mac has to work at playback time.

MODIFYING EFFECTS

You can modify GarageBand's Real Instrument settings and save them with your song. Refer to the sections "Modifying Real Instrument Settings" and "Saving Real Instrument Settings" in Chapter 4. Also we will cover creating your own Real Instruments in Chapter 8, "Making Your Own Software and Real Instruments."

RECORDING YOUR PERFORMANCE

We've covered putting together some killer backing tracks using loops, keyboards, and even electric guitars. Now it's time to look at recording real sound from Real Instruments. Whether it is your voice, an acoustic guitar, or a trumpet, GarageBand was made to record it.

THE ROOM

Where you record can be as important as what you record.

A very quiet room with very little reverberation is an ideal place to record your singing or playing.

Of course, this is not always possible. Usually, you have to record in the same room as your computer and the associated fan noise. G4s, for example, are notoriously noisy.

Also, you may live in an apartment with noisy neighbors. And convincing them to turn down Eminem, after you've been blasting Fat Boy Slim for the last week, might prove to be dicey.

The bottom line is to use common sense and do the best you can with what you've got. Here are a few tips:

- Tack some blankets over windows and doors while you are recording.
- Record in a carpeted room.
- Find a way to record during a weekday while your neighbors are at work.
- Move your mic as far away from your Mac as possible.
- Make sure your mic is facing away from noise sources.
- If possible, put your Mac's CPU inside a closet and run longer cables to your monitor and keyboard.
- Put a foam-lined cardboard box over your Mac while recording. Cut open the side of the box toward the wall so your Mac can still get cool air. And remove the box immediately after recording.

Inevitably, a dog's bark or a fire engine's siren is going to ruin that perfect take. But preparing your recording space will lead to fewer blown takes and more quiet, good ones.

LAYING DOWN THE TRACK

We've already recorded using a mic in the section "Changing Effects After Recording," earlier in this chapter. But let's go over it again step by step from beginning to end.

We'll assume that you have your mic and headphones hooked up with your speakers off and that you have set your recording levels:

1 Launch GarageBand and create a new song by selecting File ⋯⟩ New.

2 Select a key that you would like to sing in and name the song `Vocal test 2`.

3 Click Create.

4 Click New Track to bring up the New Track window, and click Real Instrument.

5 Select Vocals and the effect preset of your choice. Set the Monitor radio button to On.

6 Click OK to create a new track.

7 To use a metronome while recording, choose Control, Metronome.

8 To hear a one-measure count-in before recording, select Control ⋯⟩ Count In.

9 Move the playhead to where you want to begin recording. Click the Record button (R) to begin recording.

10 Sing or play something.

11 Click Play to turn recording off and pause playback.

12 Click Go to Beginning to return to the start of the song.

13 Click Play to play back what you just recorded.

tip

Record only a portion of a song—that is, a verse, a chorus, or a solo—with each recording pass. This will give you much more flexibility in editing regions and tracks.

Notice that you created a region when you recorded. You can manipulate the region you just created like any other region. See the section "Manipulating Regions" in Chapter 2, "Making Music with Apple Loops."

If you are unhappy with your recording, you can erase the track by selecting the region(s) in the track's timeline and pressing the Delete key. To only replace a portion of your recording, move on to the next two main sections in this chapter, "Editing Your Performance" and "Overdubbing Your Performance."

EDITING YOUR PERFORMANCE

One of the cool things about GarageBand is that you don't have to be a perfect singer to get a near-perfect recording. All it takes is a little editing and overdubbing.

Just like when you recorded your guitar in Chapter 4, when you recorded with a microphone, you created what GarageBand calls a *Real Instrument track*. You'll notice that the track regions are a purple color. As far as GarageBand is concerned, all Real Instrument tracks are the same. A guitar Real Instrument track is the same as a vocal instrument track which is the same as a didgeridoo Real Instrument track.

The Real Instrument track that you just recorded is exactly the same as the guitar Real Instrument tracks from the last chapter, in that your track editing options are rather limited. In fact, in the Track Editing window the only thing you can edit is the selected region's name.

You can, however, perform all of the region manipulations to the track in the track editor that you can in the timeline. These include splitting and joining regions. The usual edit functions of cutting, copying, and pasting can be performed both in the timeline and the Edit window. Editing by manipulating regions in the track editing window is covered in depth in the next chapter's section titled "Track Editing Real Instruments."

note

In Chapter 9, "Making Your Own Loops," we'll show you techniques to turn your Real Instrument tracks into Real Instrument loops for more editing flexibility.

OVERDUBBING YOUR PERFORMANCE

Overdubbing techniques for vocals and other Real Instruments are exactly the same as for the guitar Real Instrument tracks that we discussed in Chapter 4. Refer to the section "Overdubbing Your Guitar" in Chapter 4 for a full explanation of overdubbing techniques that you can use for vocals or other instruments.

RECORDING A BLUES TUNE

For our blues tune, we're going to cheat a little bit. Rather than build the backing tracks up from scratch, like we did in the previous chapters, we are going to use one of the Apple tutorial songs that came with the iLife DVD to provide our backing band. That way we can concentrate on just recording some vocals over the track.

LOADING "SHUFFLIN' GUITAR BLUES"

Go ahead and dig out the iLife '04 Install DVD so that you can copy the GarageBand demo songs to your hard drive.

If you already copied the songs, you can obviously skip this step.

1 Insert the iLife '04 DVD.

2 Drag the GarageBand Demo Songs folder to your hard drive. If you are short on hard drive space and don't want to install all of the demos songs, open the GarageBand Demo Songs folder on the DVD. Then open the G3 Projects folder on the DVD. Drag the Shufflin' Guitar Blues song to your hard drive.

3   Go ahead and eject the DVD and return it to its safe storage place.

4   Double-click the Shufflin' Guitar Blues song on your hard drive to open it.

5   Click play to hear the song.

Next we'll write some lyrics for this song.

GOT THEM LYRIC WRITIN' BLUES

Willie Dixon we're not. We aren't even in the Belushi league. But here goes:

> (verse)
>
> Got off work 'bout half past four
>
> Couldn't wait to get home and play some more
>
> Don't need no drummer in a deep blue funk
>
> a bass that's been arrested, or a tuba that's drunk
>
> I gotta brand-new axe and it's on my Mac
>
> I'm so dang happy I'll never go back
>
> (chorus)
>
> Now I'm a one-man garage band
>
> I'm a one-man garage band
>
> (verse)
>
> don't need nobody to gimme a hand
>
> gonna send this song out across the land
>
> Gonna send it out across the Internet
>
> It's a wonder I ain't a big star yet

Of course, we know you can write something better, but at least we have something to work with for the purposes of this tutorial. If you are a female, you can substitute *one-woman* for *one-man*, to avoid gender confusion in your audience or feel free to write your own lyrics to go with the song.

LAYING DOWN THE REFERENCE TRACK

You've got backing tracks, you've got lyrics, and all you need now is your voice to make it a song. Take a look at the following sidebar for some performance tips.

We're providing some sample lyrics that you can use to record a vocal track if you can't come up with any lyrics on your own. It beats singing, "Doobie doobie doo, blah, blah, blah blah." However, it's up to you to give it your own vocal style.

Play the demo song a few times and experiment with the lyric lines, belting out different melodies. When you're starting to feel comfortable with the tune, go ahead and give recording a shot.

PERFORMANCE TIPS

Here are a few tips to help you get your best singing performance when recording with GarageBand:

- **Get a helping hand**—Find somebody who can manage clicking Record and other GarageBand functions, so that you can concentrate on singing.
- **Stand up**—Your whole vocal tract works better when you're standing.
- **Print out the lyric sheet**—If you can't read hand-scrawled lyrics, you might be singing "There's a bathroom on the right" instead of "There's a bad moon on the rise." Also wear your glasses. Save the beauty contest for the stage.
- **Use a music stand**—Using a music stand to hold your lyric sheet when recording avoids ruining a take due to a paper rustle. Also make sure you have a pencil handy so you can write down changes and notes.
- **Have liquid handy**—Tea, water, or whatever works for you. But remember that the song never sounds as good on a hangover.
- **Monitor at reasonable levels**—If you blow out your hearing, you won't be able to sing very well.

It's a good idea to start by singing the whole song through once to have a reference track and to get a feel for the flow of a song. Don't worry about getting things perfect, you just want to get through the entire song.

Let's record:

1. Click New Track to bring up the New Track window.

2. Click Real Instrument, and select Vocals and the effect preset of your choice.

3. Set the Monitor radio button to On and click OK to create a new track.

4. To use a metronome while recording, select Control ⸱⸱⸱⟩ Metronome.

5. To hear a one-measure count-in before recording, select Control ⸱⸱⸱⟩ Count In.

6. Move the playhead to the beginning of the song, and then click the Record button (R) to begin recording.

7. Sing the song the whole way through.

8. Click Play to turn recording off and pause playback.

9. Click Go to Beginning to return to the start of the song.

10. Click Play to play back what you just recorded.

Go ahead and save the song as **One Man Band** or a similar name. Now we have a reference track to work with. If you knocked out the tune exactly like you wanted, you're done. Go have a cocktail, or beer, or cuppa tea. However, if it's not quite perfect yet, let's work on overdubbing the song to get your best performance.

OVERDUBBING FOR PERFECTION

We still need a little work to get the song to where it can be heard by other humans, without them commenting on how much we sound like William Shatner when singing.

Luckily, we can perfect any part of our performance without affecting the rest of it by recording a replacement part in a new track.

For our song, we are going to overdub the verses of the song on one track and the chorus on another. Let's start with the first verse:

1 Click New Track to bring up the New Track window.

2 Click Real Instrument, and select Vocals and the effect preset of your choice.

3 Set the Monitor radio button to On and click OK to create a new track.

4 To use a metronome while recording, select Control ⸺⸗ Metronome.

5 To hear a one-measure count-in before recording, select Control ⸺⸗ Count In.

6 Click Mute on your reference track.

7 Click Cycle.

8 Drag the cycle region so that it covers from the beginning of the measure before you started singing to the beginning of the measure just past where you end the first verse. This is to give us room on both ends of our recording. We call these *handles*.

9 Click Record and then sing the first section of the song.

10 GarageBand automatically stops recording at the end of the cycle region and starts cycling in Play mode (see Figure 5.4).

FIGURE 5.4
This figure shows the results of our first overdub.

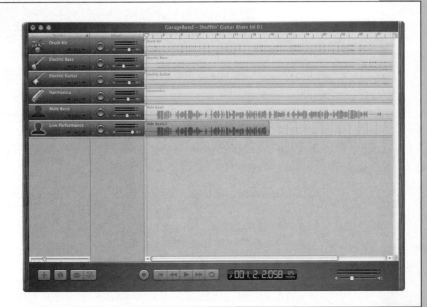

Next, we'll use another track to overdub the chorus part of the song:

1 Click New Track to bring up the New Track window.

2 Click Real Instrument and then select Vocals and the effect preset of your choice.

3 Set the Monitor radio button to On and click OK to create a new track.

4 Drag the cycle region so that it covers from the measure before you started singing the chorus to the beginning of the measure just past where you ended the chorus. This is to give us one-measure handles on both ends of our recording.

5 Click Record and then sing the chorus section of the song.

6 GarageBand automatically stops recording at the end of the cycle region and starts cycling in Play mode (see Figure 5.5).

FIGURE 5.5
This figure shows the results of our second overdub.

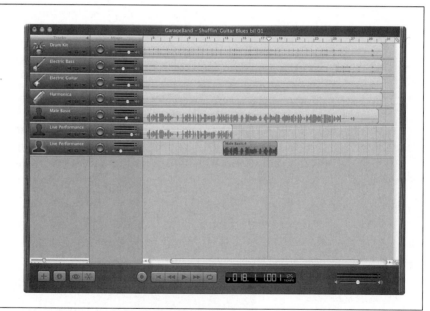

Now let's go back to our first overdub track to record the second verse/outro part of our song:

1 Click the track with our first overdub to select it. Double-check that you have the proper track selected.

2 Drag the cycle region so that it covers from the measure before you started singing the second verse to the end of the song.

3 Click Record and then sing the second verse section of the song.

4 GarageBand automatically stops recording at the end of the cycle region and starts cycling in Play mode (see Figure 5.6).

FIGURE 5.6
This figure shows the results of our third overdub.

5 Click Cycle to turn off the cycle region. Then click Go to Beginning to return to the start of the song.

Play back the song. If you are unhappy with the results you can go back and re-record any of the regions that you want. If you are happy with the results, it's a good idea to go back through the Track Info windows for your tracks and turn off monitoring, so that you don't get any surprise feedback.

At this point, you can add more tracks, delete your reference track, or edit your performance using region editing.

Be sure to save this song for future reference and so that all of your hard work is not lost.

In the next chapter, we'll go deeper into editing and mixing your songs to give them that final polish.

caution

Audio feedback can cause hearing damage. Make sure that track monitoring is turned off on all tracks after recording with mics.

6

EDITING AND MIXING YOUR MUSIC

Once you've finished recording your song, you can take it from ordinary to extraordinary by carefully editing, arranging, and mixing.

Editing can take care of small mistakes or add variety to your tracks. Arranging the tracks and regions of your song can add interest or even extend your song. Mixing is where you add effects and set the volumes and pans for your tracks so that they blend together to become a cohesive song.

While we can't promise you miracles, we can at least show you some very clever sleight of hand to make your song sound miraculous.

EDITING AND ARRANGING REGIONS

You are probably pretty familiar with basic region manipulation by now. In this section, you're going to learn to use the track editor to slice, dice, and arrange Real Instrument regions like a Ginsu master.

Up till now, we've been manipulating regions in the timeline. For Software Instruments, using the timeline to manipulate regions is the way to go. This is because, for Software Instruments, the Track Editor is oriented toward the powerful note editing features we covered in the section "Editing Software Instruments Using the Track Editor" in Chapter 3, "Recording Your Own Music with Software Instruments."

But for Real Instruments, we can use the Track Editor to perform the same region manipulations that we've been doing in the timeline with greater accuracy and control.

IN THIS CHAPTER:

➤ Learn advanced techniques for editing and arranging regions

➤ Find out how to optimize your track effects to get the most out of GarageBand

➤ Master the use of a master track to add effects and control the volume of your song

➤ Learn how to use some of these techniques to mix a rock song

TRACK EDITING REAL INSTRUMENTS

Let's go and visit an old friend. Launch GarageBand, and then open the Guitaro song that we created in Chapter 4, "Recording Your Guitar," and let's see what we can do with a little editing.

If you don't have the song saved, you can create a new song, select A as the Key, and name it `Guitaro`.

THE PLAYHEAD LOCK

Before we start editing, we want to introduce you to the playhead lock. If you look in the lower-right corner of the timeline, you will notice two small triangles that sort of look like two miniature playheads stacked on top of one another. If you click this icon, the triangles will no longer be stacked on top of one another.

This unlocks the timeline and Track Editor playhead from each other so that the timeline and Track Editor can now show different parts of the song. However, the playhead can now scroll offscreen.

If it is in the locked position, GarageBand tries to keep the playheads for both the editor and the timeline centered in their respective windows and it is the song that scrolls under the playheads.

Play the song through a couple times while locking and unlocking the playheads to see how this works.

In the Guitaro song we had the drum loop `Live Edgy Drums 11` start at measure 5 of the song. And then the loop continues through the entire song. It serves the purpose, but we can add a little more life to it. First let's add an intro bit to it:

1   Open the Loop Browser.

2   Select the Drums button and then select Rock/Blues in the pane on the right side.

3   Scroll down to the `Modern Rock Drums 07` loop and drag the loop to measure 4 of the drum track on the timeline.

Now we have a drum intro/fill to work with, but we need to only use the last half of the loop, so that we end up with a half-measure-long drum fill:

1   Click Track Edit to open the Track Editor.

2   For our purposes, let's move the playhead to the start of measure 4 and unlock the playheads (see Figure 6.1).

3   Click the `Modern Rock Drums 07` region on the timeline to select it if it is not already selected.

The Playhead lock

FIGURE 6.1
Our old friend, the
Guitaro song, with the
playhead lock set to the
unlocked position.

4 Drag the Zoom slider in the Track Edit window to about the middle of
its range so that the selected Modern Rock Drums 07 region spans
most of the edit grid.

Now we are set up so that we can split the region in half to get our half-
measure drum fill.

There are three ways to split the region:

- Move the playhead to the middle of the region, in this case measure 4
  beat 3, and select Edit ⋯⟩ Split.

- Move the playhead to the middle of the region, in this case measure 4
  beat 3, and press ⌘-T.

- Click-drag to select the region in the waveform display of the Track
  Editor, in this case between measure 4 beat 1 and measure 4 beat 3.

The drag-select method allows you to perform very precise splitting of
regions without disabling the Snap to Grid feature. Go ahead and split the
region using the drag-select method, and then press the Delete key to
delete the now-selected first half of the region.

Play the first few measures of the song. Now we have a more natural drum
intro to the song.

To give the song yet more interest, let's cut and paste a half-measure-long
drum fill onto the drum track right before the chorus parts of the song.

tips

Grab the area
between the
timeline and
the Track Edit
window and drag upward
to expand the Track Edit
window.

When Snap to Grid is
activated in the Control
menu, the following
snaps to the nearest grid
value set in the timeline
ruler button: dragging
loops to the timeline,
moving regions, resizing
regions, moving the play-
head, moving the cycle
region, and moving con-
trol points on the volume
and controller curves.

ON MEASURES AND BEATS

In music, time is usually measured in measures and beats rather than minutes and seconds. Just as you could have a ruler where an inch is divided into tenths rather than sixteenths, the number of beats in a measure is defined by the time signature.

By far the most common time signature is 4/4, which means that the measure is divided into four quarter-note beats.

Musicians find their place in the timeline of a song by using the measures and beat measurement. For example, measure 17 beat 3 is halfway through the 17th measure in the song.

Move the playhead to measure 4 beat 3 in the waveform display of the Track Editor. Slowly move your cursor over the region. Notice that the cursor changes as it rolls over various areas of the region:

- The upper-left corner of the region changes the cursor to a vertical bar with both left- and right-pointing arrows next to it. Clicking and dragging with this cursor allows you to move the entire region.

- The upper-right corner of the region changes the cursor to a vertical bar with a circular arrow next to it. Clicking and dragging with this cursor allows you to extend the region as a loop.

- The lower-left corner of the region changes the cursor to a vertical bar with a left-pointing arrow next to it. Clicking and dragging with this cursor allows you to extend the region to the left, (if possible).

- The lower-right corner of the region changes the cursor to a vertical bar with a right-pointing arrow next to it. Clicking and dragging with this cursor allows you to extend the region to the right, (if possible).

- Over most of the region, the usual state of the cursor is a cross-hair shape. Clicking and dragging with this cursor allows you to select any area from a small portion of a region to several regions. Clicking after selecting splits the region or regions at the start and end points of the selection.

tip

You can type in values in the Time display to move the playhead to a precise location. Just double-click the value that you want to change and type the new value.

To copy the entire region, do the following:

1 Click in the upper-left corner of the region to select the entire region.

2 Copy the region by pressing ⌘-C.

3 Move the playhead in the Track Editor to measure 12 beat 3.

4 Paste the region by pressing ⌘-V.

5 While we have the region in the copy buffer, paste the region at measure 24 beat 3 and measure 36 beat 3.

6 Play the song to hear the drum fills.

We are getting something closer to what a real drummer would play, although maybe a drum fill to get us out of the choruses would be cool, too. A slightly different drum fill would even be cooler:

1 Move the playhead to measure 17 beat 1 in the song.

2 Paste the drum fill region.

3 In the track edit waveform display, click in the lower-left corner of the newly pasted region and drag to expand the region to the left.

4 The expanded region now starts at measure 16 beat 3. Like a Kiss comeback tour, you'll notice that we brought back the first half of the original Modern Rock Drums 07 region, so that now we have a one-measure-long drum fill spanning from measure 16 beat 3 to measure 17 beat 3 (see Figure 6.2).

FIGURE 6.2
Our new and expanded drum fill.

Play the song and you will notice our new drum fill sounds a little weird because it is hanging over into measure 17.

In the track edit waveform display, click in the lower-right corner of our newly expanded region and drag to contract the region to the left from measure 17 beat 3 to measure 17 beat 1.

Notice that we now have a half-measure gap in the drum track from where we had pasted the drum fill over measure 17, before we resized it. Don't freak! We'll fix it.

In the track edit waveform display, click in the lower-left corner of the region that we pasted over that now starts at measure 17 beat 3 and drag to expand the region to the left. Look! No more gap.

Look at Figure 6.3 to see the results of this operation.

FIGURE 6.3
Now our song has dual drum fill action!

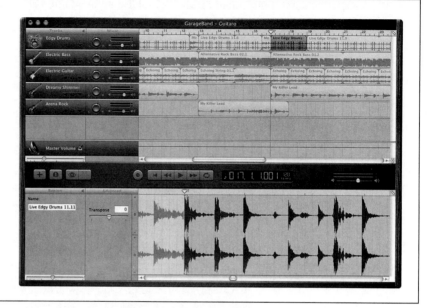

Play the song to hear our changes. Also, we really should save the song by selecting File ⸱⸱⸱⸱⟩ Save at this point.

Let's do one more copy-and-paste operation to this song so that we end up with the same drum fill at the end of the second chorus as the first chorus:

1 Move the playhead to measure 13 beat 1.

2 Slide the Zoom slider in the Track Editor all the way to the left, so that you can see at least measures 13–17 in the waveform display.

3 Shift-select the two regions that make up the first chorus of the song, starting at measure 13 beat 1 and measure 16 beat 3.

4 Copy the regions by pressing ⌘-C; then move the playhead to measure 25 beat 1. Paste the regions by pressing ⌘-V, so that now the second chorus has the same drum fill at the end as the first chorus.

Play the song. Cool, huh? By just adding one drum fill loop and editing it, we now have a drum track that sounds like something a real drummer would play with fills at the beginning of the song and then just before and at the end of the chorus sections of the song. Be sure to save the song because we'll be mixing it later in the chapter.

OPTIMIZING TRACK EFFECTS

The term *effects* in recording is short for audio special effects. Of course, everybody just uses the shortened form today. Strictly defined, an effect is anything that changes the sound from its original form. However, more loosely defined, the term is applied to audio signal processing hardware or software.

While GarageBand's built-in effects can add a lot to your songs, they also take a heavy toll on your Mac's processing power. If you have a G5 double-pumper, you'll probably never notice, but if you have G3 or a less-powerful G4, you need to know how to streamline your effects in order to get more tracks and fewer errors from GarageBand.

It's easy in GarageBand to keep adding tracks to a song using a variety of Real and Software Instruments without realizing that the effects that are part of each of your instruments are bringing your Mac to its knees.

Let's take a look under the hood at these effects to see what we can do to eliminate some effects while still keeping your tracks sounding great.

note

We cover effects and effect settings in Chapter 8, "Making Your Own Software and Real Instruments."

WHERE ARE THE EFFECTS?

If your Mac's performance is suffering, you might want to get an idea of how many effects a particular track is using and discover which tracks are dragging your song down. To access these effects, we need to open the Track Info window for an existing track. Let's take look at some of the effects in our rock song Guitaro:

1. Open the Guitaro song that we worked on in the previous section.

2. Double-click the Electric Bass track to bring up the Track Info window for the track.

3. Click the triangle labeled Details in the lower-left corner of the window.

4. The Track Info window expands to show the effects for a particular instrument. Figure 6.4 shows the effects for our Electric Bass track.

FIGURE 6.4
The Electric Bass track hardly has any effects at all.

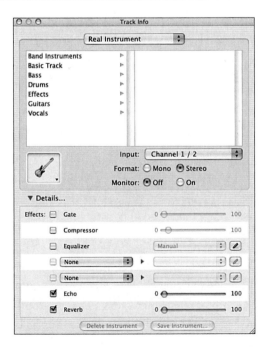

Notice that bass track has only a small amount of echo and reverb. Let's browse through some of our other tracks.

With the Track Info window still open, click the Dreamy Shimmer guitar track. As you can see, Dreamy Shimmer uses a lot of effects. This is an example of a track that could use a diet. Figure 6.5 shows the effects for the Dreamy Shimmer guitar track.

FIGURE 6.5
The Dreamy Shimmer track went super-size in the effects department.

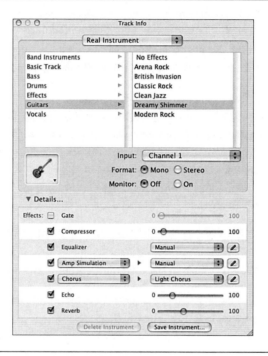

KEEPING THE ECHO AND REVERB

Echo and reverb are *master* effects. That means that all the tracks send their signals via the Reverb slider in the Track Info window to the master track's echo or reverb effect.

So, if one track is sending a signal to the reverb, it's pretty much the same as all tracks sending signals to the reverb. The master effect's settings are controlled in the master track. The only way to gain significant performance is to turn off echo and reverb in the master track. And hopefully you can avoid doing that.

We'll look at the master track in this chapter, but the bottom line is to try turning off effects other than echo and reverb in the Track Info window.

ELIMINATING UNNECESSARY EFFECTS

Think of eliminating effects as downsizing a company. It would be better to keep everyone around, but sometimes we just can't afford to.

The best way to determine which effects are contributing a lot to your song and which are not is to play through the song, try different instruments for each track,

tip

The playhead changes color to indicate how much of your Mac's processing power GarageBand is using. The triangle changes from white through orange to red as the processor use increases.

and then try clicking on or off the various effects that make up the instrument on a track. Once you have created a "light" version of an instrument that works, go ahead and save it by clicking the Save Instrument button in the lower-right corner of the Track Info window.

For example, try deselecting the compressor and equalizer effects for the Dreamy Shimmer instrument and then save the instrument as `Dreamy Light`.

The "light" instrument doesn't sound too different from the original, yet every effect that you eliminate will help the performance of your Mac.

CHOOSING MASTER TRACK EFFECTS

You learned to adjust the volume curve of the master track to create a fade-out back in Chapter 2, "Making Music with Apple Loops," but that only scratched the surface of what the master track can do for a song.

The master track controls several things for the overall song:

- The key, tempo, and time signature of the song
- The overall volume of the song at any point
- The type of echo and reverb effect applied to a song
- The amount of compression and equalization effect applied to the entire song
- An additional selectable effect which can be applied to the overall song

Let's take a look at the master track effects settings:

1 Open the `Guitaro` song if it's not already open.

2 Select Track ⋯⟩ Show Master Track, if it is not already visible.

3 Double-click the master track's speaker icon to bring up the Master Track Info window.

4 Click the triangle labeled Details in the lower-left corner of the window.

The Track Info window expands to show the master effects. Figure 6.6 shows the default master Track Info window.

Notice that, just like Software and Real Instruments' Track Info windows that have a two-column pane that contains instrument categories on the left and an instrument list on the right, the master Track Info window contains musical genres on the left and, once you select a genre, a preset list appears on the right.

Clicking Rock in the left column and LA Rock in the right column brings up the preset shown in Figure 6.7.

tips

Click the Solo button on a track while a song is playing to try different instrument and effect settings.

You can change the key, tempo, and time signature of a song in the master Track Info window.

FIGURE 6.6
The master Track Info window has control of your entire song.

FIGURE 6.7
The master Track Info window with LA Rock selected as a master effect (aka the Red Hot Chili Peppers effect).

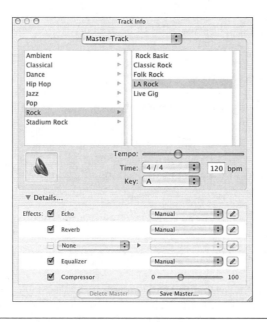

Play the song through several times while selecting different effect presets to get an idea of how they affect the overall sound of the song.

We'll take a closer look at all of the individual effects that make up GarageBand instruments and master effect presets and show you how to make your own instruments in Chapter 8.

In the next section of this chapter, we'll mix our rock song so that we can export it to iTunes and share it with the world.

MIXING A ROCK SONG

The purpose of mixing a song is to balance all of the separately recorded elements and to mix them into a cohesive whole. There probably are as many ways to mix a song as there are people to mix it.

In this section we'll put some of the things you've learned so far to the test by using the track volume and panning controls, track volume curves, setting effects, using the master track effects and volume curve, setting the end of song marker, and setting the final output levels.

While this section shows you the elements that go into mixing a song, how you mix it is up to your own creativity and taste.

> **note**
>
> The type of echo and reverb are set in the master Track Info window. The amount of echo and reverb are set in the instrument's Track Info window.

VOLUME AND PANNING

Volume and panning are what gives dimension to a mix. If you close your eyes and imagine a band on stage, the various instruments would be closer or further away from you and the instruments would be spread out from left to right across the stage.

By using volume to move things backward and forward in a mix and panning to locate things from left to right in a mix, we create a virtual sound stage.

SETTING MAXIMUM SAFE LEVELS

The most obvious part of mixing is twiddling with the volume sliders to create a mix of the various instruments, where each can be heard and none are overpowering.

This can be quite subjective and leads to the "Mo' Me" syndrome, where each member of the band thinks that his part is getting buried in the mix.

We'll just stay out of this conflict and show how to adjust the volume of the various tracks. Let's start our mix by setting the volume of the bass track:

1. Open the Guitaro song if it's not already open and click Solo (the button with the headphone-shaped icon) on the Electric Bass track.

2. Click the play button.

3. While the song is playing back, carefully adjust the volume slider for the Electric Bass so that the track level meter only occasionally goes into the yellow or red zones. And most definitely not so high as to light the red clipping lights to the right of the track level meters (see Figure 6.8).

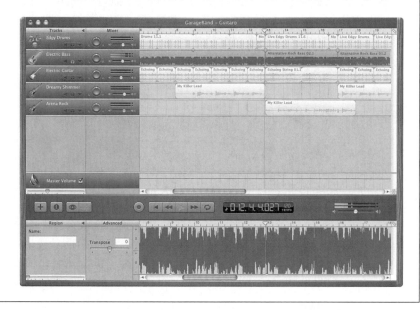

FIGURE 6.8
Setting the track volume level is a tight wire between hot enough and too hot.

tips

Set up a cycle region the length of the song to cycle playback while you are mixing.

There are many opinions on how to go about mixing a song. The method of mixing that we are showing is a subtractive method where you set maximum "dry" levels first, add effects, and then rebalance your levels.

4. If the red dots next to the level meters light while the track is playing, turn down the volume level slider by dragging it slightly to the left, and try playing the track again.

5. Once you have a level set for the bass, let's add the drums to the mix. Click Solo on the drum track so that both the bass and drum track Solo buttons are lit.

6. Double-click the drum track's instrument icon to bring up the Track Info window for the track.

7. Select the No Effects instrument for the drum track, and then click Cycle to begin cycling playback of the song.

8. While the song is playing back, carefully adjust the volume slider for the drum track so that the track level meter only occasionally goes into the yellow or red zones. And most definitely not so high as to light the red clipping lights to the right of the track level meters.

Now, we'll go ahead and repeat the level setting process with our rhythm guitar track:

1. Click Solo on the rhythm guitar track so that the rhythm guitar, bass, and drum track Solo buttons are lit.

2. Click Cycle to begin cycling playback of the song.

3. While the song is playing back, carefully adjust the volume slider for the rhythm guitar track so that the track level meter only occasionally goes into the yellow or red zones. And most definitely not so high as to light the red clipping lights to the right of the track level meters.

What we are doing at this point is setting the *maximum safe* levels for each track without effects applied. As we proceed with the mix and add effects, you will only have to move the volume sliders a little from these settings.

Repeat the process of selecting No Effects in their respective Track Info windows and setting the maximum safe level for the two remaining tracks.

Also at this time, uncheck the Master Volume check box if it is checked and set the master volume slider the same way that we set the individual track levels. Figure 6.9 shows all tracks without effects and set to maximum safe levels.

FIGURE 6.9
All the tracks are at equal volume levels, at least according to the volume level meters.

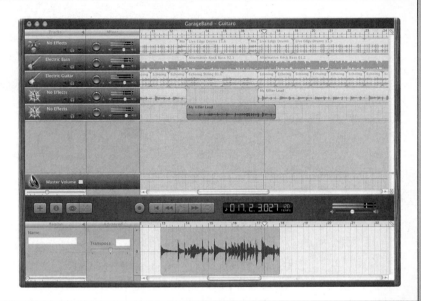

SETTING UP PANNING

Thinking back to our virtual sound stage, we want to place the instruments of our band from left to right on the stage. Drums are usually in the center of the stage toward the back with, in our case, the bass guitar, rhythm guitar, and lead guitar spread across the rest of the stage. Let's use GarageBand's pan knobs to give our mix some space:

1 First, go ahead and click all of our tracks' Solo buttons so that they are all off. Click Cycle to start cycling the playback of our song.

2 Locate the pan knob, which is just to the right of the track level slider for the bass track. Click the pan knob for the bass and drag it right until the knob rotates to about the 2 o'clock position.

3 Click the pan knob for the rhythm guitar and drag it left until the knob rotates to about the 10 o'clock position.

4 Let's leave the lead guitar tracks in the center of the mix for the moment. Take a look at Figure 6.10 to see our current pan settings.

tip
Pan an equal number of instruments to the left and right to keep a balanced mix.

The pan knob

FIGURE 6.10
We panned the bass to the right and the rhythm guitar to the left to give a little spread to our mix.

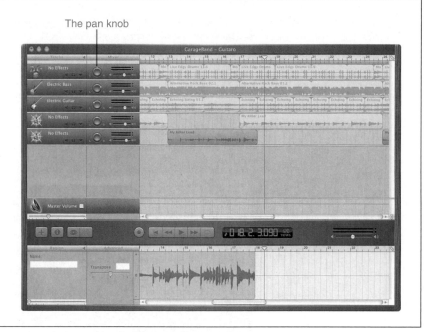

Let's move on to the fun stuff, adding effects!

ADDING EFFECTS TO YOUR MIX

Like chocolate syrup on ice cream, everybody loves adding effects to a mix. GarageBand has a great selection of time-tested, professionally designed effect combinations called Real Instruments. But like a hot new car, these instruments are begging to be modified and customized. Let's have some fun.

tip

Always make sure that any effect you add to a mix is adding to rather than detracting from the song's appeal.

1 Click Solo for the drum track and then click Cycle to start cycling the playback of our song.

2 Double-click the drum icon to bring up the Track Info window for the drum track.

3 Click the Details triangle in the lower-left corner of the Track Info window.

Although we could spend all day going through all of the Real Instrument presets to find just the right preset, for the purposes of this tutorial, let's keep things simple by selecting No Effects and just adding a little reverb.

note

Don't limit yourself to just the one instrument category in the Track Info window. A vocal preset may be just the thing for your drum track.

Grab the Reverb slider at the bottom of the Track Info window and slide it to the right until it's at about 40% of the maximum.

Notice that, with this particular effect, we haven't affected our track volume level.

Go ahead and click Play to pause playback.

Let's save this effect as a Real Instrument.

Click Save Instrument in the lower-right corner of the Track Info window.

When the Save Instrument window appears, name the instrument **Just Damp** and click Save (see Figure 6.11).

FIGURE 6.11
Hey y'all, watch this! We're about to save our own Real Instrument.

Congratulations, you just created your first Real Instrument.

Click the drum track's Solo button to off and click Play to hear the entire mix.

Next, let's add effects to the verse track of the lead guitar:

1. Click the track's icon to select it. Select Dreamy Shimmer in the Track Info window. While this sounds pretty good with the track, we want to modify it slightly.

2. In the Track Info window, to the right of the Amp Simulation effect, click the pop-up menu labeled Manual and select British Lead (see Figure 6.12).

3. On the guitar that we recorded, this effect sounds awesome so let's save the instrument for posterity. Click Save Instrument in the lower-right corner of the Track Info window.

4. When the Save Instrument window appears, name the Instrument **British Shimmer** and click Save.

Notice that according to the track's level meter, this effect actually reduced the volume level for this track. But for the moment, don't adjust the track's level.

Let's move on to the track with the chorus and solo lead guitar parts.

Click the track's icon to select it and then select Arena Rock in the Track Info window.

We love this instrument for this part, so let's go with it.

We've got a pretty awesome mix going here. We don't want to lose our work so far, so we had better save our song as **Guitaro Mix 01**.

caution

When adding effects, keep a close eye on the track volume level and reduce it if necessary.

FIGURE 6.12
Is British Lead heavier than American Lead?

USING THE MASTER TRACK

So far we've hit a little bit on how to use the master track to perform a fade-out throughout the book. Also we looked at master track effects earlier in this chapter. Let's set our master effects, put a fade-out at the end of our song, and see what the master track can do for our mix.

We already set our master track effects setting to LA Rock earlier in this chapter, but let's open the master Track Info window to confirm our settings.

1 Select Track ····⟩ Show Master Track, if it is not already visible.

2 Double-click the master track's speaker icon to bring up the master Track Info window.

3 Make sure that Rock is selected in the left effects category pane and that LA Rock is selected in the right effects list pane. If they're not, go ahead and select the LA Rock effects preset.

4 Next, let's go ahead and click to enable the Master Volume check box to enable the volume curve for the master track.

5 Scroll to the end of the song to see if we still have a four-measure fade-out starting at measure 45. If not, click to create a control point on the master track volume curve at measure 45. Create another control point at measure 49 and drag it downward to create our fade-out.

A fade-out and some effects are all we needed to do with the master track for this song. Let's put some finishing touches on our mix.

FINISHING TOUCHES FOR YOUR GARAGEBAND MIX

Let's put on a final coat of wax and buff up our mix so that it's ready to export to iTunes.

Remember that we noticed that the verse lead guitar part was a little low in the mix; well, now is the time to fix it:

1 Click Play to start cycling playback of the song.

2 Drag the track volume slightly to the right to bring up the track's volume. Make sure that the volume meter doesn't go into the red zone or that the red clipping indicators to the right of the track volume level meters don't light.

3 You can also bring up the volume on the other lead guitar part slightly.

Also keep in mind that mixing is a creative process and that you want to tailor your mix to the style of the music. You might want to emphasize guitars in a speed metal tune, put the drums out front in an electronic dance tune, or pull the drums back and emphasize vocals in a ballad. Let's set the final output volume of our song mix:

1 While the song is playing back, carefully adjust the Master Volume slider so that the master level meter only occasionally goes into the yellow or red zones. And most definitely not so high as to light the red clipping lights to the right of the track level meters.

2 If the red dots next to the level meters light while the track is playing, turn down the input level slider by dragging it slightly to the left.

3 Click Play to pause playback, reset the output level meter, and try playing the track again.

Once we have our master output levels set, it's time to introduce you to the mysterious end-of-song marker:

1 Scroll the timeline window all the way to the right. Notice the purple left-pointing triangle in the beat ruler bar. Meet Mr. end-of-song marker.

2 Drag this little purple fellow to the end of your song in the beat ruler.

3 Now, turn off the cycle region for the song by clicking Cycle.

4 Click Go to Beginning and click Play to start the song.

Let it play to the end and the playhead will stop at the end-of-song marker rather that just continue scrolling. Cool, huh?

Figure 6.13 shows our mix playing back; notice the level meters and the end-of-song marker.

tips

Clicking Play to pause playback resets the output level clipping indicators. Reclick Play to continue playback.

To only export a part of the song, set the cycle region to cover the part of the song that you want to export. You can also export silence or perhaps an echo ring out at the end of your song by moving the cycle region beyond the end of the song.

The end of song marker

FIGURE 6.13
The Guitaro mix in all
of its glory.

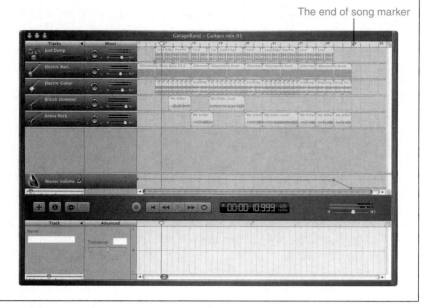

Be sure to save this song as **Guitaro mix 01** for future reference and so that all of your hard work is not lost.

You can also download a copy of the Guitaro 01 song from `http://macaudioguy.com/gbb/downloads/`.

In the next chapter, we'll show you how to export your songs to iTunes and share them with the world.

FINISHING UP

7

I f a Mac user makes a GarageBand song and no one is around to hear it, does it still make a sound?

It's time to take the song out of GarageBand and spread the joy.

You can do this a variety of ways, all starting with an export to iTunes. From there, you can burn a CD, transfer it to your iPod, upload it to the Internet, or use your song in other iLife applications.

EXPORTING TO ITUNES

The first step to using your song outside of GarageBand is to export it to iTunes.

PERFORMING THE EXPORT

Ready to perform the complex task of exporting your song to iTunes? Okay. Then open one of your songs, select File ·····⟩ Export to iTunes.

That's it. That's all you need to do. There aren't even any options to consider.

A progress dialog box appears with the words `Creating Mixdown` in it. You will see the timeline behind that scroll to the right as the song is processed. Figure 7.1 shows what your screen might look like.

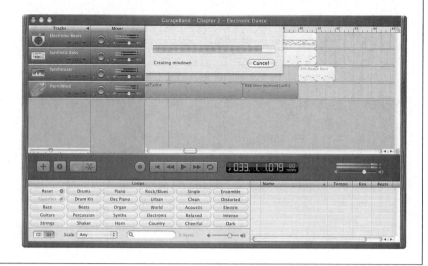

FIGURE 7.1
Your song is making the leap from GarageBand to iTunes.

The process might take a long while, depending on the length and complexity of your song.

When it is done, iTunes automatically opens. However, you might not see your song right away. In practice, iTunes just opens up to the last view you were using. So, you might see your Abba collection rather than your song.

But if your iTunes music collection is empty, you should see something like Figure 7.2, depending on your iTunes viewing preferences at the moment.

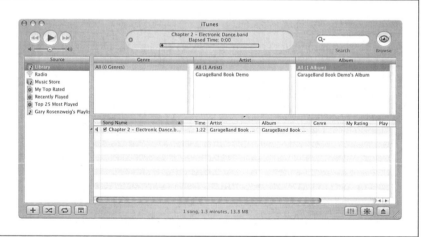

FIGURE 7.2
The iTunes window with your soon-to-be-hit song.

Notice that GarageBand created an artist, in this case GarageBand Book Demo. In your case it would be your username. It also created an album, which would use your username as well.

If you exported more songs from GarageBand, they would all be filed under this same artist and album.

To play the song once it is in iTunes, simply select it in the list and click the large Play button at the top of the iTunes interface. You can also double-click the song.

WHERE IS THE SONG, REALLY?

When you exported from GarageBand, two things happened. The first was that the song was mixed and exported into an AIFF file, which is a standard sound format. Then, iTunes took this file, indexed it, and added it to the iTunes library.

The location of the file that GarageBand created depends on your iTunes settings. If you have your iTunes Advanced preferences set to Keep iTunes Music Folder Organized, then the `.aif` file for the song will be named with the name of your song and placed in an artist and album folder that corresponds to your GarageBand Export preferences.

However, if you do not have this option in iTunes set, then GarageBand does not know exactly where you want the song saved. So, you will find it as `Bounced.aif` in the `Music:iTunes:iTunes Music:Import` folder under your user directory.

You can find the iTunes Advanced preferences by selecting iTunes ⋯⟩ Preferences ⋯⟩ Advanced in iTunes. You will find the GarageBand Export preferences by selecting GarageBand ⋯⟩ Preferences ⋯⟩ Export in GarageBand. The latter will let you customize the artist, album, and playlist name that iTune uses for each exported song.

If you have worked with raw sound files before, you know that you can take this AIFF file and edit it in a variety of sound editors.

note

Why `Bounced. aif`? A *bounce* is an old audio industry term for a recording that combines several tracks together.

BURNING TO CD

Once you have accumulated several tracks, you may want to burn your own audio CD. You don't need any additional software to do this, as iTunes comes complete with a CD creation solution.

What you will need, however, is a CD burner. Most Macintosh computers sold today come with either a Combo Drive or a Super Drive. The first reads both CDs and DVDs and burns CDs. The second also burns DVDs.

If you have an older Mac, you will need to upgrade your CD drive or buy an external CD burner to make CDs.

To create an audio CD, follow these steps:

1. Select File ⋯⟩ New Playlist. While you can use iTunes to listen to any song or album by selecting it, you can only burn CDs from a playlist. You can also use the playlist that GarageBand created when you exported your song.

2. Select the new playlist in the Source listing at the left side of the iTunes window. It is named `untitled playlist X`. Rename it to whatever you want your CD to be called.

3 Return to your iTunes library by selecting Library in the Source list.

4 Find your songs and drag them to the playlist name in the Source listing. This adds those songs to that playlist.

5 Select the playlist in the Source listing so you can view the songs inside it. Confirm that those are the songs you want to put on the CD. You can also select and drag them to rearrange the order of the CD or select one and press Delete to remove it.

6 The large button in the upper-right corner of the iTunes window should now say `Burn Disc`. Click it.

7 The message area at the top of iTunes now flashes `Please insert a blank disc...`. So, go ahead and insert a blank disc.

8 You will get another message at the top of the window that says `Click Burn Disc to Start`. So, you need to click the same button a second time.

iTunes creates the CD, which could take a few minutes. When it is done, it mounts the CD on your desktop and in the iTunes Source list as an audio CD. You can test it out right away or eject the disc to play it elsewhere.

MAKING AN MP3 FILE

Take a look at the file size of the `Bounced.aif` file—it's huge. Even a short song can be several megs in size. A typical 5-minute AIFF song will take up about 45MB of drive space.

Select the song in iTunes and select File ····⟩ Get Info. You will get a window like Figure 7.3. It shows you a variety of information about the song.

FIGURE 7.3
The Summary tab of the information window shows us that this 18-second song takes up a whopping 3.1MB!

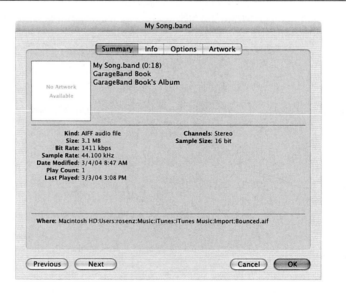

If you want to share your song with others via your iPod or by sending it to them via the Internet, you will want to trim the file size down. The standard way of doing this is to convert it to an MP3 file.

MP3 files include more than just the audio itself. They also include information about the song, such as the title, album, artist, and so on.

By default, iTunes uses a format called Advanced Audio Coding (AAC) rather than MP3. Technical experts will note that ACC is actually a type of MP4 file, the successor to MP3. AAC files encode audio at a higher quality and have some antipiracy features built in for use by the music industry. But many people still use the term *MP3* to refer to all compressed audio files, whether they are MP3 or AAC.

You don't have to use AAC when converting your files. iTunes lets you select AAC, MP3, AIFF (`.aif`), or WAV as your encoding option. In iTunes, select iTunes ⤑ Preferences and then select the Importing tab. You will get the window shown in Figure 7.4.

> **note**
>
> An MP3 file is a compressed format for audio files. It is the main format in addition to AAC used by iTunes when you rip songs from your CD collection. It is also the main format used by people who share their music over the Internet.

FIGURE 7.4
The iTunes Importing preferences allow you to select the format and quality setting.

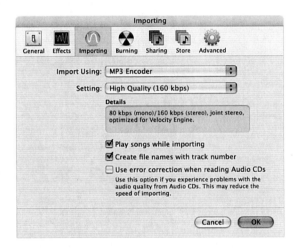

The formats each have their own uses:

- **MP3**—MP3 makes sense if you want a universal format to use when sharing files on the Internet.
- **AAC**—Using AAC gives you slightly better quality and works well with iTunes and iPods—but not with most non-Apple MP3 players.
- **AIFF**—Your exported file from GarageBand is already in AIFF format, so there is no need to convert it. AIFF is the raw format used by most Mac audio editors.
- **WAV**—WAV is the raw format used by most Windows audio editors.

note

Both MP3 and AAC files are much smaller than their AIFF and WAV counterparts.

To convert your song to the compressed AAC format, select it in iTunes and select Advanced ⟶ Convert Selection to AAC. The actual menu choice may read Convert Selection to MP3 if you have your iTunes ⟶ Preferences ⟶ Importing ⟶ Import Using preference set to MP3 instead of AAC. After a short delay for processing, you will see a second copy of your song appear in iTunes.

You can also select the bit rate setting for the conversion. The AAC default is 128Kbps, which is good quality for AAC. If you are using MP3, 160Kbps is fine for most uses.

When you select the information for this second copy, you get a summary that looks like Figure 7.5.

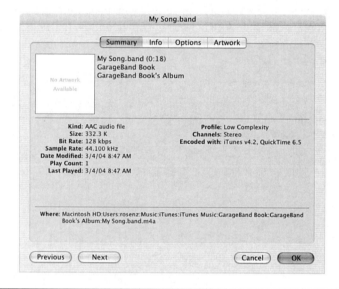

FIGURE 7.5
The information window tells you that this song is AAC encoded and takes up much less disk space than its `.aif` counterpart.

note

The smaller file size of an AAC file versus an `.aif` file is a huge advantage of AAC files. But keep in mind that you are sacrificing some quality. However, it is hard for most people to hear the difference between AAC files and the original unless they have fantastically expensive audio equipment. Try to hear the difference yourself.

Now that you have an AAC version of your file, you will probably want to remove the `.aif` version from iTunes. Just select it and press Delete. However, you may want to save this `.aif` file and use it if you want to create higher-quality audio CDs. Remember that the original `.aif` file is always better quality than any MP3 or AAC file.

The information window in Figure 7.5 also shows you where the file for the song is located. You can see that the AAC version is actually placed in a different place than the `Bounced.aif` file. It is even given the name of your original GarageBand song.

The file extension `.m4a` is used for AAC files. You'd think that they would use `.aac`, but not so. If you used MP3, you would get a file with a `.mp3` extension.

This new version of your song is slimmer and more versatile than the old `.aif`. You are now ready to transfer the song to your iPod and share it over the Internet.

MOVING SONGS TO YOUR IPOD

Transferring songs to your iPod can happen in one of two ways. If you use the default iTunes and iPod settings, then your iPod is set to automatically synchronize files with iTunes every time you connect your iPod.

Using the default settings, all you need to do is plug your iPod in and let iTunes do the work. When the synchronization is complete, your songs will be on your iPod. They will be listed just as they were in the iTunes browser.

However, if you have your iPod set for manual updating, then you must drag the songs from your library or playlist to the iPod icon in your Source list.

Transferring your songs to your iPod is that easy. In fact, it is exactly the same process that you would use to transfer your ripped music or purchased music to your iPod.

SHARING YOUR MUSIC ON THE INTERNET

Once you have created a .m4a or .mp3 version of your song, you can easily share it on the Internet in a number of ways.

MAKING YOUR SONG AVAILABLE ON YOUR .MAC ACCOUNT

If you are a .mac subscriber, you can put your music files up on your .mac home page. Doing so is relatively easy and can actually be done almost completely in the OS X Finder.

Currently, there are very easy ways to use both iPhoto and iMovie to upload pictures and movies to your .mac account. It is quite possible that Apple is working on a way to quickly and easily upload music from GarageBand as well. But until then, you can use the iDisk/File Sharing capabilities of your .mac account to share your music.

If you already have a Web page set up to show the contents of your iDisk Public folder, then uploading new content there is easy:

1. Open your iDisk in the Finder. You can do this by selecting Go ⋯⟶ iDisk ⋯⟶ My iDisk. (You might already have set up various shortcuts and other ways of accessing your iDisk; if so use that method instead.)

2. Drag and drop your .mp3 or .m4a file to your Public folder in your iDisk.

That's it. Thefile is now available on your .mac Web site.

If this is your first time using your .mac iDisk Web site, then you will need to set it up first:

1. Log on to your mac.com account. Go to http://mac.com/ and enter your ID and password.

2. Locate and click the link for the Homepage feature of .mac. The interface of .mac is likely to change and evolve, so you will have to search for the list of .mac features and find the Homepage option.

notes

Switching your iPod from automatic updating to manual updating is done by Control-clicking the iPod in the Source list.

For maximum compatibility, .mp3 is the way to go. A .m4a file works for all up-to-date Macs with QuickTime 6.5 installed. But Windows XP users won't be able to use it easily, unless they have iTunes for Windows installed.

note

You can also give out your .mac Homepage URL, which should look like `http://homepage.mac.com/username/`. On that page there are links to your File Sharing page as well as other content, like any photo albums you have uploaded from iPhoto.

3 Once you are in your Homepage section, select the File Sharing option.

4 At this point, if you have never enabled file sharing before, you will be asked to select a theme.

5 Now a copy of the .mac File Sharing Web page will come up, with results varying depending on the theme you chose. At the top, you will see an Edit button. Click Edit to change the title and description of the page. You can see the page in edit mode in Figure 7.6.

6 Click Publish.

7 After you click Publish, you will be shown the URL, or Web address, of the page. It should look something like `http://homepage.mac.com/username/FileSharing1.html`. This is the URL that you can send to friends so they can see your music.

FIGURE 7.6
The Graphite theme for the .mac File Sharing Web page. You can see one song, which corresponds to the contents of your iDisk Public folder.

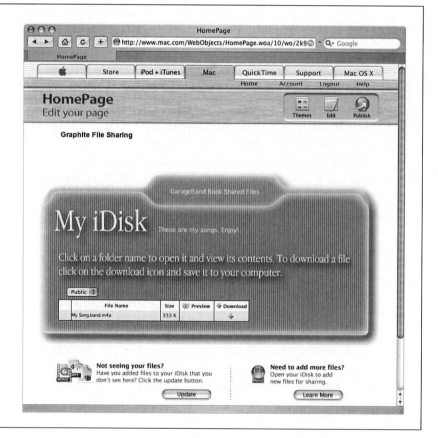

Once you have a File Sharing page set up, all you need to do is add and remove content from your iDisk Public folder to change the contents of the page.

A standard iDisk account currently comes with 100MB of space. That's room for an album's worth of music and then some.

ADDING MUSIC FILES TO YOUR WEB SITE

Do you have a Web site? Are you familiar with terms like FTP? Then sharing your music is as easy as uploading the converted `.mp3` or `.m4a` files to your site.

If you do know how to upload files to your site, then you can place your `.mp3` or `.m4a` files (remember, `.m4a` is the file type used for AAC files) there and the rest of the world will have access to them.

One method is to create a new directory on your Web site and place all of your files in there. For instance, you can create a `music` directory. Then, when a surfer goes to that directory, they will get a listing of the files in that directory.

I changed the title of the song from `My Song.band.mp3` to `mysong.mp3` to make it easier for the server to handle. In general, it is not a good idea to have files on your server with spaces in the name. It is also a good idea to stick to only one file extension.

You could also place your music at the main directory level and link to it from any page. You may want to tell users on the page that they can click the links to download the song.

EMBEDDING YOUR SONG IN A WEB PAGE

Placing a link to your song file on your site is one way to share your files; however, a more polished approach is to embed the music into a Web page so visitors can play the file right from your site.

Embedding files requires a little more HTML programming. You'll use the `EMBED` tag to allow the user to hear the song while remaining on your Web page. Here is an example:

```
<EMBED src="mysong.mp3">
```

When you use this code in a Web page, you get a small control strip that appears on the page. The user can pause the song and move the playhead. Figure 7.7 shows an example of what the page would look like.

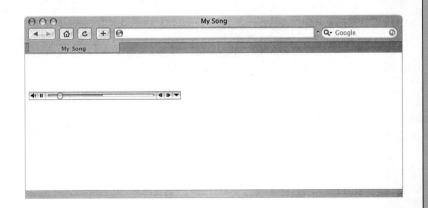

FIGURE 7.7
In Safari, the EMBED tag places a simple set of playback controls on the page from which the user can control the song playback.

tip

In some cases, security on the server would be set so that a surfer can't see a directory listing. In that case, you need to create an HTML file that links to each song. A link would look like

```
<A HREF="music/
mysong.mp3">My
Song</A>
```

This also works in other browsers, such as Internet Explorer on Windows. The user gets a Windows-looking set of controls, but with more or less the same functionality.

The EMBED tag has several other parameters you can set. Here is a list:

- autostart—If set to true, the song starts to play immediately. Some browsers may respond to the autoplay parameter as well.
- hidden—If true, the control does not appear at all.
- loop—If true, the song repeats.
- volume—Set to a value from 0 to 100 to set the starting volume.
- width/height—Controls the size of the playback controls. Setting the width is common, but setting the height only adds blank space above and below the controls. On Windows, it forces a black playback area above the controls that is not needed because there is no video portion.
- border—Works on some browsers, such as Safari, to put a black border around the controls.

So, if you wanted to have a piece of looping background music on your Web page, you could do this:

```
<EMBED src="mysong.mp3" autostart=true hidden=true loop=true>
```

If you are concerned about backward compatibility with old browsers, you can use the NOEMBED tag to show them a message:

```
<NOEMBED>The music cannot play because your browser doesn't support the embed
➡tag. You may be able to hear the music by clicking <A HREF="mysong.mp3">
➡here</A>.</NOEMBED>
```

There is no reason why you can't place a whole list of MP3 playback controllers on one page. Just be sure to set them all to autostart=false so they don't all try to play at once when the page loads.

With some spiffy graphics and a good design, you can make a nice page for people to come and hear your music.

USING YOUR SONG WITH OTHER SOFTWARE APPLICATIONS

The music you create with GarageBand can either stand alone as pieces of musical entertainment or can be used for other purposes. For instance, a game development shop may use GarageBand to compose music for its games.

Three other pieces of software in the iLife collection—iPhoto, iMovie, and iDVD—can take advantage of GarageBand compositions. In addition, other popular software can use them as well.

USING GARAGEBAND MUSIC IN IPHOTO

iPhoto, part of iLife, is software for people who use digital still cameras. While iPhoto is all about visual images, it has one feature that uses music: the slideshow.

In iPhoto, you can select some or all of your photos and click the Slide Show button at the bottom of the interface. At that point you can choose music to accompany your slideshow. By default, some quiet classical pieces are listed. But you can also choose any song from your iTunes collection, including songs you have exported from GarageBand. Here's how to do it:

1 Launch iPhoto and switch to Organize mode. Select as many photos as you want.

2 Click Slide Show, which is the second button from the left at the bottom of the screen. The Slideshow window appears.

3 Select the Music tab and you will get a window like Figure 7.8.

FIGURE 7.8
The Slideshow settings allow you to pick a classical masterpiece or one of your own.

4 Using the Source pull-down menu, select either iTunes Library or a playlist that includes your GarageBand songs.

5 Select the song you want to use from the list and click Play.

That's it. The slideshow will now play with your music in the background. Your photos and your music: very artistic.

USING GARAGEBAND MUSIC IN IMOVIE

Another iApp that can use a little music from time to time is iMovie. This software is primarily for people who use a digital video camera to take home movies and then transfer those movies to their Macs for editing.

While a tutorial on how to use iMovie could easily fill its own book, adding GarageBand music from iTunes is fairly straightforward.

First, let's assume that you have a movie clip already imported and added to the iMovie timeline. To add the music, you would do the following:

1　Switch to the timeline viewer by selecting View ⋯▸ Switch to Timeline Viewer.

2　Click the Audio button found in the row of buttons to the right side of the iMovie interface.

3　Using the pop-up menu found at the top of the right side of the iMovie interface, select either iTunes Library or a playlist that contains your songs. Figure 7.9 shows the iMovie interface this way.

4　Select the song you want to import from the list.

5　Position the playhead in the timeline at the bottom of the screen so it is where you want the music to start and then click Place at Playhead.

The music imports into iMovie and is layered with the existing audio that might already exist as part of your video clips.

Now, instead of using predictable clip-art music for your movies, you can compose a new song for every one you make.

tip

If you really want to make it sound professional, you can plan to make your movie first, note its length, and then compose a piece of music to match that length.

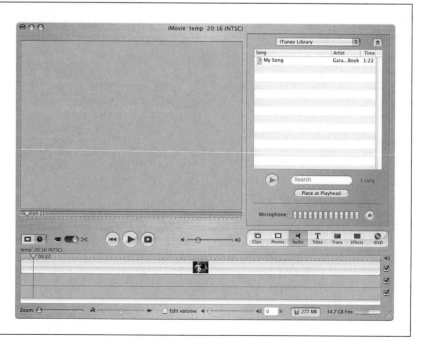

FIGURE 7.9
Your iTunes song is ready for import. So, now you can take over the music industry and Hollywood.

USING GARAGEBAND MUSIC IN IDVD

If you use iDVD to build your own DVDs, then you probably already know that you can use music in a lot of different parts of the process. For instance, you can use a looping piece of music on the title screen.

The process for getting your GarageBand music into iDVD is basically the same as it is for iMovie and iPhoto. You can bring in any music from your iTunes library, in fact.

For instance, if you want to use a GarageBand song for the background music to a slideshow, all you need to do is this:

1 After creating your slideshow, click Customize at the bottom of the window. You can see this and other iDVD buttons in Figure 7.10.

FIGURE 7.10
The iDVD interface allows you to select iTunes music in the side panel.

Audio well

2 Select Media at the top of the side panel.

3 In the pop-up menu near the top of the side panel, select Audio.

4 Find your song in the iTunes Library or a playlist. Drag the song to the Audio well at the lower-right side of the window. In Figure 7.10 it has an icon of a page with a musical note in it.

That's it. Your slideshow now plays with your custom tunes. To insert audio on the title screen or a menu screen of your DVD, it is even easier. Follow the same steps as you did for adding tunes to a slideshow, but just drag the song to the main video window area.

If you ever want to remove music from the title screen or a slideshow, just drag the icon in the Audio well out of the Audio well.

note
You can also drag the song's file from the finder to the Audio well. In fact, you can drag any audio file to it, not just ones in your iTunes library.

note

If you have a Windows program that doesn't use .aif or .mp3, chances are it uses .wav files. You can change your iTunes preferences to convert your song to a .wav file instead of a .mp3 file. PowerPoint uses .wav sound files best. In general .wav is your best bet for most Microsoft and Windows software.

USING GARAGEBAND MUSIC IN OTHER APPLICATIONS

Using your finished GarageBand music in other programs is relatively easy. You just need to use the Export to iTunes function and then grab the .aif file it generates. Alternatively, you could use iTunes to convert it to MP3 and use that as well.

Most Mac sound editors can use .aif files and most can now read .mp3 files as well. In addition, many Windows sound editors can use both formats.

Programs like Macromedia Flash and Macromedia Director can read any of these formats.

MAKING YOUR OWN SOFTWARE AND REAL INSTRUMENTS

Nothing is more unique to GarageBand than its concept of Software and Real Instruments. One thing that is really awesome about GarageBand is that it gives you the ability to create both Software and Real Instruments.

Remember that Real Instruments modify sound generated outside of GarageBand like your voice, a guitar, or a sound file. Software Instruments use your Mac's processing power to act as a sound generator for the instrument and don't rely on an external sound source.

We have actually already created a couple of Real Instruments in Chapter 6, "Editing and Mixing Your Music." In this chapter, we'll create Software Instruments, too.

USING GENERATORS

Both Real and Software Instruments in GarageBand use a combination of several effects as part of the instrument. Software Instruments also have another component called *generators* that create sound that Real Instruments don't possess. A Software Instrument's generator is responsible for actually creating the basic sound characteristics of a particular Software Instrument. That basic sound is then modified by its effects settings, just like a Real Instrument.

GarageBand includes 18 powerful generator modules with which to build instruments, as well as a "bonus" generator that has been on your Mac since QuickTime 5.

But wait, there's more! You can even use third-party Audio Unit instruments as generators in GarageBand. Not bad considering that a single hardware MIDI sound module can cost hundreds of dollars.

THE BUILT-IN GENERATORS

Let's take a tour of all 18 of GarageBand's Software Instrument generators and explore their capabilities:

1 Open a new song in GarageBand and call it **Instrument test**.

2 Double-click the Grand Piano icon to bring up the Track Info window.

3 Click the Details triangle in the lower-left corner of the window. Click the Echo and Reverb check boxes to disable the effects.

4 Click Save Instrument and name the instrument **Genny** (short for "generator" in case you were wondering); then click Save to save the instrument.

Figure 8.1 shows our newly created Software Instrument.

FIGURE 8.1
Creating a new Software Instrument is easier than pie.

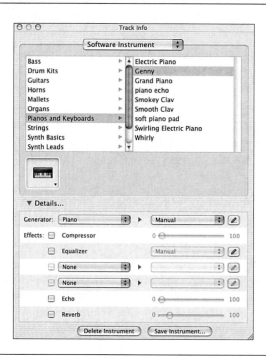

Next click the button with a pencil icon to the right of the Piano and Manual pull-down menus; we'll call this button the edit button.

The Piano generator edit window will appear. If we try to select Grand Piano from the pull-down menu at the top of the Piano generator edit window we get a Save dialog like the one shown in Figure 8.2.

FIGURE 8.2
Nag, nag, nag. Unchecking the Never Ask Again box speeds up our generator tour.

Clicking Never ask again will dismiss this box and speed up your exploration of GarageBand's generators. However, if you decide that you do want to keep seeing this dialog, click Don't Save whenever it appears in the course of our tour.

Let's take a look at the Piano generator edit window (see Figure 8.3).

FIGURE 8.3
The Piano generator edit window allows you to edit the piano. Editing a real piano usually involves an axe.

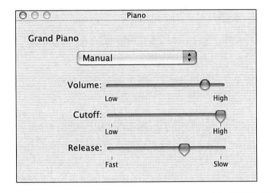

At the top of the window is a pull-down menu that allows you to choose from ready-made presets or different sampled instruments or to save a preset of your own making. All of the generator edit windows have this menu. So, for simplicity's sake, we won't keep mentioning it as we look through the generators.

The Piano generator is a sample playback module and therefore has only a few editable parameters:

- The Volume slider controls the overall volume of the piano.
- The Cutoff slider controls how "dark" or "bright" the piano sounds. Think of it as a treble control.
- The Release slider controls how long the piano continues to sound after you release the musical keyboard key.

Next, go to the Generator pull-down menu in the Track Info window and select Strings.

Notice that the generator edit window is now titled Strings (see Figure 8.4).

note

According to Victor Hookstra, who runs the garagedoor.com Web site, GarageBand's piano generator was sampled from a rare 9-foot Yamaha CFIIIS Concert Grand Piano.

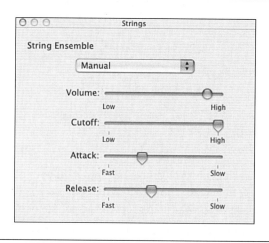

FIGURE 8.4
The Strings generator edit window is very much like the Piano edit window.

tip

Experiment by playing your keyboard while adjusting parameters in the generator edit window.

note

Note that within each generator module there may be several sampled instruments. For example, the Bass module has five different sampled basses under its preset pull-down menu.

The Strings generator is also sampled and, like the Piano, only has a few parameters:

- The Volume, Cutoff, and Release sliders work similarly to the piano's parameters of the same name.
- The Attack slider controls how quickly the strings achieve full volume once a key is pressed.

Select Horns from the Generator pull-down menu in the Track Info window.

Notice that Horns has the same parameters in the edit window as the Strings did. In fact, all of the sampled generator modules have the same three or four parameters the Piano and Strings have. Here is a list of the sample-based generator modules:

- Piano
- Strings
- Horns
- Woodwind

- Guitar
- Bass
- Drum Kits

Let's move on to the non-sampled generator modules.

Select Electric Piano from the Generator pull-down menu in the Track Info window (see Figure 8.5).

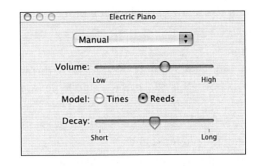

FIGURE 8.5
The Electric Piano generator edit window allows you to get that Holiday Inn entertainer electric piano sound.

The Electric Piano module is the first of the true synthesizer modules. Its parameters are

- **Volume**—This slider controls the overall volume of the piano.
- **Tines/Reeds**—These radio buttons allow you to choose between the sharper toned Tine or the mellower-toned Reed sound. These are terms left over from when electric pianos used these technologies to simulate a piano sound.
- **Decay**—This slider determines how long it takes the sound to fade away after it reaches maximum volume when a key has been pressed and held.

Select Analog Basic from the Generator pull-down menu in the Track Info window (see Figure 8.6).

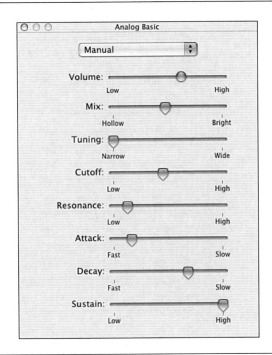

FIGURE 8.6
The Analog Basic generator is the meat and potatoes of synthesizers.

note

In synthesizer speak, the Attack, Decay, Sustain, and Release parameters are often called the *volume envelope* or the *ADSR envelope*.

The Analog Basic is an '80s style polyphonic (many notes at a time) synthesizer. Note that it has a dozen ready-made presets under its preset pull-down menu. Its parameters are

- **Volume**
- **Mix**—This slider controls the mixture of the module's two sound generators or oscillators. This allows the sound to go from a hollow sound to a brighter sound.
- **Tuning**—This slider determines the musical interval between the oscillators, allowing for a fuller sound.
- **Cutoff**—This slider controls the "darkness" or "brightness" of the sound. Think of it as a treble control.
- **Resonance**—This slider controls the harmonic richness of the sound.
- **Attack**—This slider controls how quickly the sound achieves full volume once a key is pressed.
- **Decay**—This slider determines how long it takes the sound to fade away after it reaches maximum volume when a key has been pressed.
- **Sustain**—This slider controls how long the sound stays at full volume before decaying when a key has been pressed and held.

Select Analog Mono from the Generator pull-down menu in the Track Info window (see Figure 8.7).

FIGURE 8.7
The Analog Mono generator gives you that dance club sound typified by a certain Nordic synthesizer.

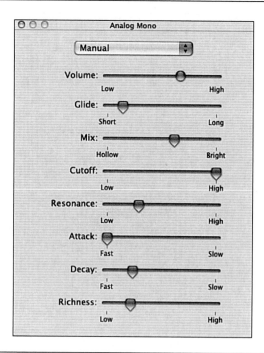

The Analog Mono is a monophonic (one note at a time) synthesizer. Note that it has 11 ready-made presets under its preset pull-down menu. Its parameters are

- **Volume**
- **Glide**—This control determines how long it takes to slide the pitch between a pressed key and a subsequently pressed key. This is often called a Portamento control. Think of a trombone.
- **Mix**—This slider controls the mixture of the module's two sound generators or oscillators. This allows the sound to go from a hollow sound to a brighter sound.
- **Cutoff**—This slider controls the "darkness" or "brightness" of the sound. Think of it as a treble control.
- **Resonance**—This slider controls the harmonic richness of the sound.
- **Attack**—This slider controls how quickly the sound achieves full volume once a key is pressed.
- **Decay**—This slider determines how long it takes the sound to fade away after it reaches maximum volume when a key has been pressed.
- **Richness**—This slider slightly detunes the oscillators from each other for a thicker, richer tone.

Select Analog Pad from the Generator pull-down menu in the Track Info window (see Figure 8.8).

> **tip**
>
> One playing technique for monophonic synthesizers is to hold down a lower note and then play the melody on higher notes. The pitch returns to the lower note between each high note, creating an interesting effect.

FIGURE 8.8
The Analog Pad generator gives you those huge pads that bring tears to the eyes of moviegoers everywhere.

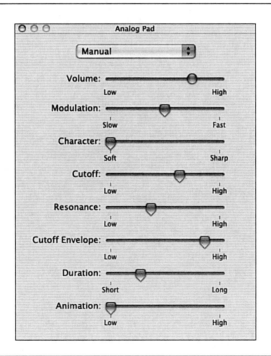

The Analog Pad is a polyphonic (many notes at a time) synthesizer that has a rich soundtrack sound; these types of sounds are often called *pads*. Note that it has a dozen ready-made presets under its preset pull-down menu. Its parameters are

- **Volume**
- **Modulation**—This slider determines the speed at which the tone of the oscillator rises and falls.
- **Character**—This slider adjusts the oscillator between a softer or sharper sound.
- **Cutoff**—This slider controls the "darkness" or "brightness" of the sound. Think of it as a treble control.
- **Resonance**—This slider controls the harmonic richness of the sound.
- **Cutoff Envelope**—This slider controls the amount of "sweepiness" in the sound by applying an envelope to the tone of the sound rather than to its volume.
- **Duration**—This slider controls the duration of the tone sweep of the sound.
- **Animation**—This slider determines how much the sound pans between the left and right speakers, as well as affecting the tone sweep of the sound.

Select Analog Swirl from the Generator pull-down menu in the Track Info window (see Figure 8.9).

FIGURE 8.9
The Analog Swirl generator sound gave movies like *Tron* that way cool futuristic sound.

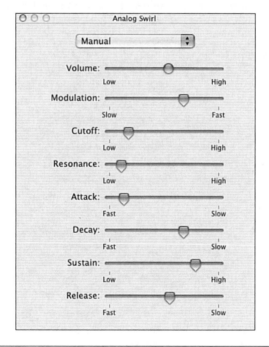

The Analog Swirl is a polyphonic synthesizer that has sweeping or swirling sound and is based on a kind of synthesis called pulse width modulation. Note that it also has a dozen ready-made presets under its preset pull-down menu. Its parameters are

- **Volume**
- **Modulation**—This slider controls the speed of the swirling sound of the oscillator.
- **Cutoff and Resonance**—These sliders control the brightness and harmonic richness of the sound respectively.
- **Attack, Decay, Sustain, and Release**—These sliders control the volume envelope of the sound.

Select Analog Sync from the Generator pull-down menu in the Track Info window (see Figure 8.10).

FIGURE 8.10
The Analog Sync generator sound gave the guitar-deprived bands of the '80s the lead sound that they needed. Think Duran Duran.

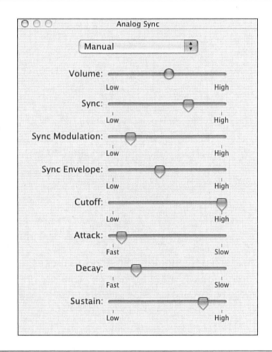

The Analog Sync is a polyphonic synthesizer that has a sharp, metallic attack sound and is good for lead parts. Note that it also has a dozen ready-made presets under its preset pull-down menu. Its parameters are

- **Volume**
- **Sync**—This slider adjusts the tonal quality of the oscillator from high to low.
- **Sync Modulator**—This slider controls the speed at which the tone of the oscillator wavers.
- **Sync Envelope**—This slider controls the amount of sweepiness in the sound by applying an envelope to the tone of the sound rather than to its volume.

- **Cutoff**—This slider controls the brightness of the sound.
- **Attack, Decay, and Sustain**—These sliders control the volume envelope of the sound.

Select Digital Basic from the Generator pull-down menu in the Track Info window (see Figure 8.11).

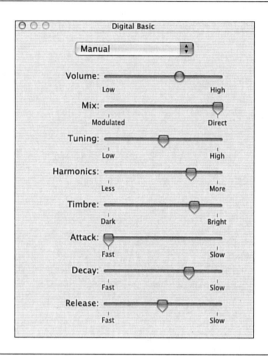

FIGURE 8.11
The Digital Basic generator is just the thing for bell-like sounds.

The Digital Basic is a polyphonic synthesizer that uses a frequency modulated (FM) synthesis technique and is good for bell-like tones. Note that it has a whopping 16 ready-made presets under its preset pull-down menu. Its parameters are

- **Volume**
- **Mix**—This slider controls how much the oscillators are frequency modulated. The more modulation the sound has, the more bell-like overtones it has.
- **Tuning, Harmonics, and Timbre**—These sliders control the overall tone of the sound, the harmonic richness, and the brightness of the sound, respectively.
- **Attack, Decay, and Release**—These sliders control the volume envelope of the sound.

Select Digital Mono from the Generator pull-down menu in the Track Info window (see Figure 8.12).

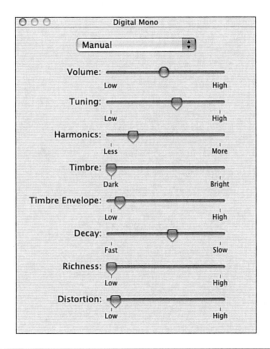

FIGURE 8.12
The Digital Mono generator can generate some cool electronic bass sounds.

The Digital Mono is a monophonic synthesizer that uses digital oscillators and is good for dance bass sounds. Note that it has 12 ready-made presets under its preset pull-down menu. Its parameters are

- **Volume**
- **Tuning**—This slider adjusts how much the oscillators are detuned. Detuning creates a fuller but harsher sound.
- **Harmonics**—This slider controls the amount of harmonic high frequencies.
- **Timbre**—This slider determines the brightness of the sound.
- **Timbre Envelope**—This slider controls the amount of detuned oscillator in the sound.
- **Decay**—This slider determines how quickly the detuned oscillator fades out.
- **Richness**—This slider adds sub-harmonics or more bass to the sound.
- **Distortion**—This slider determines the harshness of the sound.

Select Digital Stepper from the Generator pull-down menu in the Track Info window (see Figure 8.13).

FIGURE 8.13
The Digital Stepper generator is not a dancing robot, but it can sound like one.

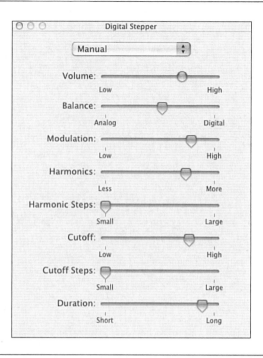

The Digital Stepper is a polyphonic synthesizer that combines a clean digital and a fat analog sound and also includes a random stepper for getting a robotic sound. Note that it has 11 ready-made presets under its preset pull-down menu. Its parameters are

- **Volume**
- **Balance**—This slider mixes between a fatter analog sound and a clean digital sound.
- **Modulation**—This slider determines if the sound has a purer or a richer sound.
- **Harmonics**—This slider controls the amount of harmonic high frequencies in the sound.
- **Harmonic Steps**—This slider controls the amount of random modulation (stepping) that affects the harmonic content of the sound.
- **Cutoff**—This slider controls the brightness of the sound.
- **Cutoff Steps**—This slider controls the amount of random modulation (stepping) that affects the tonal content of the sound.
- **Duration**—This slider determines how long the sound plays after a key has been released.

Select Tonewheel Organ from the Generator pull-down menu in the Track Info window (see Figure 8.14).

FIGURE 8.14
The Tonewheel Organ generator sound has a rich blues and R & B tradition. Sort of like the (wink, wink) Hammond B3 Organ with Leslie speaker does.

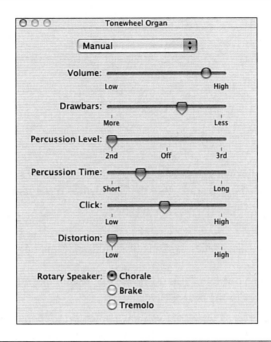

The Tonewheel Organ is a polyphonic synthesizer that has a classic B3-type organ sound. Note that it has six ready-made presets under its preset pull-down menu. Its parameters are

- **Volume**
- **Drawbars**—This slider controls the richness of the sound.
- **Percussion Level**—This slider determines the tuning of the percussion component of the organ sound.
- **Percussion Time**—This slider controls how quickly the percussion element of the sound fades out.
- **Click**—This slider controls the volume of the clicking element of the organ sound.
- **Distortion**—This slider determines the harshness of the sound.
- **Rotary speaker**—These radio buttons determine which part of the organ sound pans between the speakers.

Select Electric Clavinet from the Generator pull-down menu in the Track Info window (see Figure 8.15).

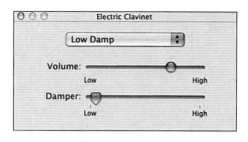

FIGURE 8.15
The Electric Clavinet generator sound is like a clavinet sound, only electric.

The Electric Clavinet is a polyphonic synthesizer that has a clavinet sound which is similar to a harpsichord sound. Note that it only has three ready-made presets under its preset pull-down menu. Its parameters are

- **Volume**
- **Damper**—This slider controls the muffling or deadening of the sound.

This concludes our tour of GarageBand's Software Instrument generator modules. We hope you enjoyed the tour. B' bye!

Just kidding. You can see that you have some pretty heavy synthesis power behind you in GarageBand. If you just saved the generator presets, you could add over 50 new Software Instruments to GarageBand. Add all the permutations of generators and effects, and the possibilities are almost infinite. Next, we're going to let you in on the secrets of the DLSMusicDevice.

THE SECRET OF THE DLSMUSICDEVICE

If you scroll down past the Electric Clavinet in the Generator pull-down menu of the Track Info window, past a grayed heading that says Audio Unit Modules, you will notice a cryptically named module called the DLSMusicDevice.

If you select this module and click the edit button, it brings up the window shown in Figure 8.16.

FIGURE 8.16
Believe it or not, there are 128 more instruments hidden in this device.

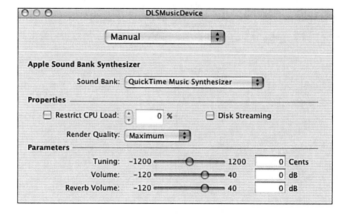

This device is actually a part of QuickTime and has been hanging around your Mac since QuickTime 5.x. The *DLS* in DLSMusicDevice stands for downloadable sound. DLS is an extension of the MIDI protocol that allows devices to download sets of sounds that can be played by a MIDI controller. These sound sets are sometimes called *sound fonts*. Without getting too much into the history of things, the DLSMusicDevice is Apple's Audio Unit sound font player and, since GarageBand recognizes Audio Unit instruments, here it is.

The problem is that—in GarageBand V1.01, at least—the device doesn't play sound fonts. Doh! It does, however, play the 128-instrument Roland General MIDI sound set that comes with QuickTime. Woo hoo! But it will only play piano unless you have a MIDI controller that can send MIDI program change messages. Doh!

Read your keyboard's documentation to see if your keyboard has a Program Change control. If it does, you're in luck. To overcome GarageBand's glaring omission of a trumpet instrument, all we have to do is set our program change number to number 57 and voilà! Trumpet.

This seems to be an answer to many a GarageBand prayer. But wait, because there is still evil afoot. If you record your newfound trumpet in GarageBand and then save the song, you might be in for a surprise when you reopen the song. Your beloved trumpet will have turned back into a piano. Woe is you.

Here is probably the coolest trick in this book. When you record your trumpet, hit a quick note at the beginning of your track, and then do your program change as GarageBand is recording the track. This way, the program change command is recorded in the Software Instrument track and will be there when you reopen the song. It is magic, no?

If you take it even further, you can record several program changes on a track. So, not only could you have the number 57 trumpet, but also the number 60 muted trumpet on the same track!

While we have the Track Info window open, let's save a Software Instrument called DLS Device. Make sure that you have the DLSMusicDevice selected in the Generator pull-down menu of the Track Info window.

Click Save Instrument and save the instrument as **DLS Device**. Simple enough?

AUDIO UNIT INSTRUMENTS

In addition to the 18 built-in generators with their almost limitless ability to create instruments and the DLSMusicDevice that gives you access to 128 instruments, GarageBand allows you to access third-party Audio Unit instruments.

notes

A list of the 128 general MIDI instruments and their program numbers can be found in Appendix F, "General MIDI Instruments List."

An example song file titled DLS Demo is available at http://macaudioguy.com/gbb/downloads/.

tip

Save a Software Instrument called DLS Device with the DLSMusic device selected as the generator so you can use the DLSMusicDevice in any song you create.

note

These effects and instruments are available from developers and range in price from free to several hundred dollars.

Audio Unit is Apple's audio plug-in format that allows third-party developers to create effects and instruments for use in high-end music software like Apple's Logic products.

We'll go deeper into Audio Unit instruments and how to install them and use them and even turn you on to some cool free instruments in Chapter 10, "Advanced Techniques." For now, let's move on to GarageBand's effects.

USING BUILT-IN EFFECTS

Effects are common between both of GarageBand's types of instruments as well as with the master track.

Each Real Instrument, Software Instrument, and master track in GarageBand has a set of either four or five professional-quality effects, including:

- Gate (Real Instrument tracks only)
- Compressor
- Equalizer (EQ)
- Echo
- Reverb

Besides these effects, which all of the instruments include, there are two additional effect slots, in which you can choose from 12 GarageBand effects and another 12 Audio Unit effects that Apple has included with GarageBand to add to instruments.

Let's take a close look at all of GarageBand's included effects.

THE COMMON EFFECTS

First, let's take a look at the four effects that are common among Real Instruments, Software Instruments, and the master track, as well as the Gate effect which only appears in Real Instruments:

1 Open the `Instrument test` song from an earlier section of this chapter.

2 Create a new Real Instrument track, select Basic Track and No Effects, and click OK.

3 Double-click the No Effects icon to bring up the Track Info window for the Real Instrument track.

4 Click the Details triangle in the lower-left corner of the window.

The Track Info window will have seven rows of effects with five rows of named effects; the echo and reverb effects will have their active check boxes checked, as shown in Figure 8.17.

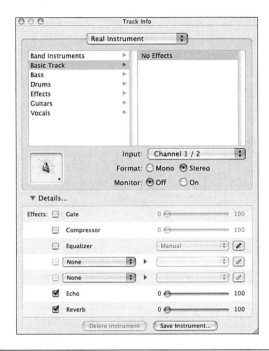

FIGURE 8.17
Our old friend the Track Info window; notice that even with No Effects, the Echo and Reverb are active. What's up with that?

GATE EFFECT

Click in the check box to activate the Gate effect. The Gate effect or, more accurately, the noise gate effect only has a slider to adjust.

A *noise gate* only allows audio to pass if it is above a certain volume level. Any sounds that are softer than that level are muted. This can be a useful effect to get rid of unwanted low-level noise on a track. But it can also cause an unwanted choppy sound. Use this effect with discretion.

The Gate slider adjusts the volume level at which sound will be muted.

COMPRESSOR EFFECT

Click in the check box to activate the Compressor effect. The Compressor effect only has a slider to adjust.

A *compressor* is an effect in which the difference between the loudest and softest parts of a track is reduced in range. Compressors are especially useful on vocal tracks where there is a great deal of dynamic range. Reducing the range of a track allows its volume to be increased so that it is more apparent in a mix.

The Compressor slider determines how much the dynamic range of a track is reduced.

tips

Hooking up a radio or other constant audio source to your Mac's audio input will allow you to hear the results of the various effects on the audio.

Gate can also be used to give drums a punchy '80s sound.

tip

You can often raise the volume level of a track after a compressor is applied.

EQUALIZER EFFECT

Click in the check box to activate the equalizer effect. Then click the effect edit button (the one with the pencil icon) to bring up the effect edit window, as shown in Figure 8.18.

At the top of the window is a pull-down menu that allows you to choose from ready-made effect presets or to save a preset of your own making. All of the effect edit windows have this menu. So for simplicity's sake, we won't keep mentioning it as we look through the various effects, other than mentioning how many presets each effect has.

FIGURE 8.18
Strangely enough, the effects edit window is very similar to the generator edit window.

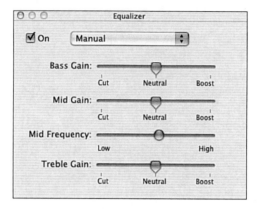

Notice that the window also has an On check box to the left of the pull-down menu. Clicking the check box On or Off is a good way to listen to how an effect affects the sound of a track.

Getting back to the equalizer, an equalizer (EQ) allows you to adjust the volume of the various frequencies that make up a sound. You can use an equalizer to add bass to a drum or treble to a vocal to make them more apparent in a mix. Overused, EQ can make a track sound unnatural or muddy.

The Equalizer effect has 16 presets. The Equalizer edit window has these parameters:

- **Bass Gain**—This slider allows you to adjust the volume of the bass frequencies of a sound.
- **Mid Gain**—This slider allows you to adjust the volume of the middle frequencies of a sound.
- **Mid Frequency**—This slider adjusts the frequency that is affected by the Mid Gain slider.
- **Treble Gain**—This slider allows you to adjust the volume of the higher frequencies of a sound.

Let's move past the two user-selectable effects slots that we'll cover soon and skip to the echo and reverb effects.

As we discussed briefly in Chapter 6, "Editing and Mixing Your Music," echo and reverb are send effects.

The amount of a track's signal that is sent to the echo and reverb is adjusted with the Echo and Reverb sliders in the Track Info window and is saved as part of an instrument.

The echo and reverb types are set for the entire song in the master Track Info window and are saved as part of the master effects.

THE MASTER TRACK EFFECTS

The master track effects are applied to all of the tracks of a song. However, the individual track's echo or reverb send amount determines how much or little of the individual track's sound is affected.

> **note**
> The master track is always active even if it is hidden.

Be careful because changing a setting in the master track will obviously change the sound of the entire song. That is what makes them dangerous and fun.

Let's explore!

1 If the master track is hidden, select Track ⋯⟩ Show Master Track.

2 Once the master track is visible, double-click the speaker icon to bring up the master Track Info window.

3 Click the Details triangle in the lower-left corner of the window.

The master Track Info window will have five rows of effects with four rows of named effects, and the echo and reverb effects will have their active check boxes checked, as shown in Figure 8.19.

FIGURE 8.19
The master Track Info window is where the echo and reverb action is.

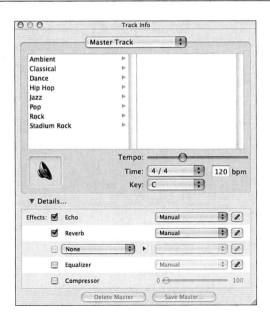

ECHO EFFECT

Click the echo effect edit button to bring up the effect edit window, as shown in Figure 8.20.

FIGURE 8.20
The Echo edit window, edit window, edit window.

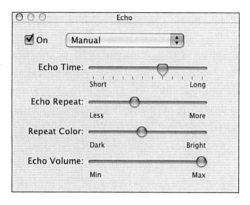

The echo effect is fairly obvious, where a sound repeats back later in time and is heard distinctly from the original sound. Echo is one of several delay effects and is sometime just called *delay*. Echo can be used to add apparent distance to a track or just because it sounds cool. Too much echo can muddy a mix.

The echo effect has 14 presets. In the Echo edit window, you can mess with these parameters:

- **Echo Time**—This slider determines how much time passes after the initial sound until the first echo is heard.
- **Echo Repeat**—This slider adjusts how many times or how long the echo repeats.
- **Repeat Color**—This slider adjusts the tone of the echo repeats.
- **Echo Volume**—This slider determines how much softer each echo repeat is from the previous echo.

REVERB EFFECT

Click the Reverb effect edit button to bring up the effect edit window, as shown in Figure 8.21.

FIGURE 8.21
The Reverb edit window has very few sliders for such a big effect.

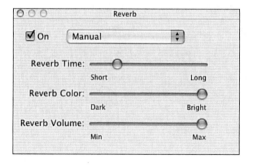

The reverb effect is often confused with echo. This is understandable, but reverb is much more complex than echo. Reverb seeks to simulate the complex echoes, reverberations, and frequency absorption of a natural space, be it a shower stall or a 50,000-seat arena. Reverb is the king of effects and has its place in practically every song and recording. Of course, too much or the wrong kind of reverb can make your song sound like it was performed in a toilet bowl.

The reverb effect has 19 presets. Should you want to create your own, you can adjust these parameters:

- **Reverb Time**—This slider adjusts the amount of time that the original sound reverberates. This often equates to the size of a space.
- **Reverb Color**—This slider adjusts the tone of the reverberation. Bright equals bathroom; Dark equals mortuary hall.
- **Reverb Volume**—This slider adjusts the amount of reverb signal that is sent to the mix. This is often set to the maximum.

OTHER EFFECTS IN THE MASTER TRACK

The equalizer and compressor effects in the master Track Info window are the same as the effects of the same name in the instrument Track Info windows. However, be aware that these effects change the overall sound of a song, not just an individual track.

You probably noticed that in the instrument Track Info windows that there are two effect slots that have a pull-down menu of assignable effects and that in the master Track Info window there is one slot for an assignable effect. Let's check out the assignable effects next.

BUILT-IN ASSIGNABLE EFFECTS

GarageBand has a selection of 12 built-in assignable effects plus another 12 Audio Unit effects that can be replaced by third-party Audio Unit effects.

In much the same manner that we toured GarageBand's generators, let's tour the assignable effects:

1 Open the `Instrument test` song from the last section of this chapter, if it's not already open.

2 Double-click the No Effects icon to bring up the Track Info window for the Real Instrument track.

3 Click the Details triangle in the lower-left corner of the window.

4 Select Treble Reduction from the assignable effect pull-down menu, as shown in Figure 8.22.

5 Click the effect edit button to bring up the effect edit window (see Figure 8.23).

note

We'll take a look at the built-in effects in this section and the Apple-supplied Audio Unit effects in the next section.

FIGURE 8.22
The Effect pull-down menu
is well endowed with
effects.

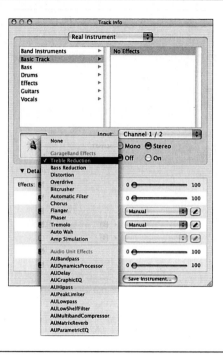

FIGURE 8.23
The treble reduction effect
is not a Star Trek episode.

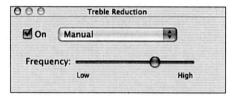

The treble reduction effect is a straightforward effect that reduces the amount of high frequencies in a sound. This effect has three presets. Its only parameter is

- **Frequency**—This slider adjusts the frequency above which the volume is reduced.

Select Bass Reduction from the assignable effect pull-down menu.

The bass reduction effect is a straightforward effect that reduces the amount of low frequencies in a sound. This effect has three presets. Its only parameters is

- **Frequency**—This slider adjusts the frequency below which the volume is reduced.

Select Distortion from the assignable effect pull-down menu (see Figure 8.24).

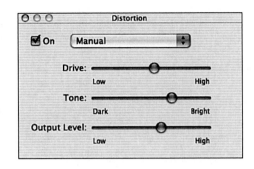

FIGURE 8.24
The distortion effect is a great way to express your inner angst.

The distortion effect is an effect that adds harshness to a sound. Distortion is good for getting a hard core sound for vocals or to "dirty up" a guitar sound. This effect has four presets. Its parameters are

- **Drive**—This slider determines how much distortion is added to the sound.
- **Tone**—This slider adjusts the tone or high frequency content of the sound.
- **Output Level**—This slider adjusts the overall volume of the effect.

Select Overdrive from the assignable effect pull-down menu.

The overdrive effect is a kinder, gentler form of distortion. Overdrive is good for getting an edgy guitar sound. This effect has three presets. Its parameters are the same as the distortion effect.

Select Bitcrusher from the assignable effect pull-down menu (see Figure 8.25).

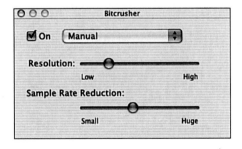

FIGURE 8.25
The bitcrusher effect can give you that cell-phone-breaking-up sound.

The bitcrusher effect creates low-bit and sample rate digital distortion. It is good for getting a tinny radio or cell phone effect. This effect has six presets. Its parameters are

- **Resolution**—This slider affects the volume range of the sound.
- **Sample Rate Reduction**—This slider adjusts the frequency content of the sound.

Select Automatic Filter from the assignable effect pull-down menu (see Figure 8.26).

FIGURE 8.26
The automatic filter effect is great for that Shaft wah-wah effect.

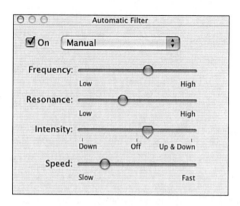

The automatic filter effect is a dynamic filter that oscillates the frequency of a sound. It is good for getting a "wah-wah" or a sweep effect. This effect has eight presets. Its parameters are

- **Frequency**—This slider adjusts the frequency center of the effect.
- **Resonance**—This slider adds harmonic overtones to the sound.
- **Intensity**—This slider determines how far the frequency center of the sound oscillates and whether the frequency only sweeps downward or both up and down.
- **Speed**—This slider sets the speed at which the frequency of the sound oscillates.

Select Chorus from the assignable effect pull-down menu (see Figure 8.27).

FIGURE 8.27
The chorus effect can make one Alanis sound like three Alanises, well almost.

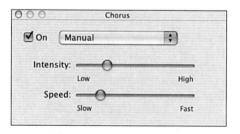

The chorus effect uses delay and detuning to make a sound fuller. It is good for getting a jazz guitar or doubled vocal effect. This effect has six presets. Its parameters are

- **Intensity**—This slider adjusts the delay of the sound.
- **Speed**—This slider adjusts the tuning of the sound from barely noticeable to warbley.

Select Flanger from the assignable effect pull-down menu (see Figure 8.28).

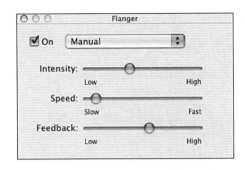

FIGURE 8.28
The flanger effect can give you a jet-airplane-is-flying-through-my-song effect.

The flanger effect is a varying delay effect that creates a whooshing or a springy sound. It is good for a sweeping strings effect. This effect has seven presets. Its parameters are

- **Intensity**—This slider adjusts the delay of the sound.
- **Speed**—This slider adjusts the speed of delay oscillation of the sound.
- **Feedback**—This slider determines how much of the effected signal is sent back through the effect, increasing its intensity.

Select Phaser from the assignable effect pull-down menu.

The phaser effect is a less-intense varying delay effect than the flanger. The phaser is good for giving stereo movement to a sound. This effect has six presets. Its parameters are the same as the flanger effect.

Select Tremolo from the assignable effect pull-down menu (see Figure 8.29).

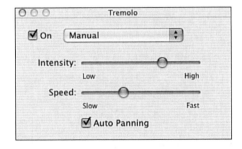

FIGURE 8.29
The tremolo effect can put the surf in your guitar or make you sound like you're really cold.

The tremolo effect is a varying volume effect. It's good for spaghetti western or surf guitar effects. This effect has eight presets. Its parameters are

- **Intensity**—This slider adjusts how much the volume of the sound varies.
- **Speed**—This slider adjusts how fast the volume of the sound varies.
- **Auto Panning**—This check box determines if the sound moves back and forth between the left and right speakers.

Select Auto Wah from the assignable effect pull-down menu (see Figure 8.30).

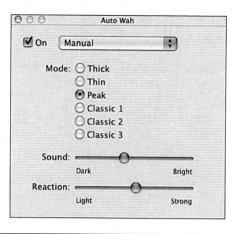

FIGURE 8.30
The auto wah effect has absolutely nothing to do with a Canadian province.

The auto wah effect is a varying frequency effect that has a randomly varying sound. It's good for a funk bass or to add tonal variation to a track. This effect has nine presets. Its parameters are

- **Mode**—These radio buttons select the intensity and the frequency of the "wah-wah" effect.
- **Sound**—This slider adjusts the overall tone of the sound.
- **Reaction**—This slider determines the frequency that the effect is applied to.

Select Amp Simulation from the assignable effect pull-down menu (see Figure 8.31).

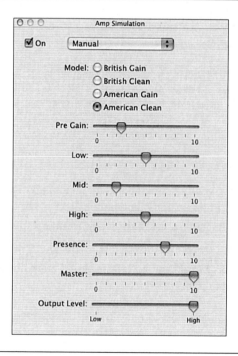

FIGURE 8.31
The amp simulation effect can save you hundreds of dollars in guitar amplifiers.

The amp simulation effect is an acoustic modeling effect and is designed to simulate the characteristics of a guitar amplifier. It's good for, well, simulating a guitar amplifier. This effect has five presets. Its parameters are

- **Model**—These radio buttons select between several simulations of amplifiers. Hint: American equals Marshall; British equals Fender.
- **Pre Gain**—This slider adds more distortion to the amp sound.
- **Low, Mid, and High**—These sliders determine the tone of the sound.
- **Presence**—This slider determines the amount of overtones in the sound.
- **Master and Output Level**—These sliders let you control the volume of the total effect and the overall volume, which gives you more opportunities to add distortion to the sound.

Spend some time exploring the built-in effects presets and parameters, and soon you'll want to make them part of your bag of tricks when creating music in GarageBand. Before we get into creating and saving your own instruments, we want to briefly go over GarageBand's included Audio Unit effects.

AUDIO UNIT EFFECTS

In addition to GarageBand's 12 built-in effects, Apple has included another 12 Audio Unit effects.

The Audio Unit effects are professional-level effects that are also available to other Mac music and audio software. Therefore, some of the names of the effects and their parameters are more cryptic than the effects that were specifically created for GarageBand.

caution

Using Audio Unit effects can have a negative impact on your Mac's performance.

In this section, we'll briefly go over these included effects and tell you what they are for without bogging us down by getting into the specifics of all of their parameters.

The 12 included effects are

- **AUBandpass**—This effect is a filter effect that allows a band of frequencies to pass while cutting higher and lower frequencies.
- **AUDynamicsProcessor**—This effect is a compressor/limiter effect that controls the volume dynamic range of a sound.
- **AUDelay**—This effect is a delay effect that allows you to create echo or other delay effects.
- **AUGraphicEQ**—This effect is an equalizer effect that allows you to raise or lower the volume level of 31 separate frequency bands.
- **AUHipass**—This effect is a filter effect that allows high frequencies to pass while cutting lower frequencies.
- **AUHiShelfFilter**—This effect is a filter effect that allows you to raise or lower the volume of high frequencies.
- **AUPeakLimiter**—This effect is a compressor effect that limits volume peaks to a preset level.

Some third-party Audio Unit effects are ports from other plug-in formats, don't conform exactly to the Audio Unit standard, and may not perform as expected in GarageBand.

- **AULowpass**—This effect is a filter effect that allows low frequencies to pass while cutting high frequencies.
- **AULoShelfFilter**—This effect is a filter effect that allows you to raise or lower the volume of low frequencies.
- **AUMultibandCompressor**—This effect is a compressor/limiter effect that lets you compress the dynamic range of multiple variable bands of frequencies.
- **AUMatrixReverb**—This effect is a reverb effect with extensive control over the reverb sound.
- **AUParametricEQ**—This effect is an equalizer effect that controls both the frequency and bandwidth to be boosted or cut.

Now that you know more than you ever wanted about GarageBand's generator modules and effects, we can move on to actually creating instruments.

CREATING AND SAVING SOFTWARE INSTRUMENTS

To create a Software Instrument, you don't really have to do anything more than select a generator preset and click the Save Instrument button in the Track Info window.

But to create a sophisticated Software Instrument, you'll want to customize generator parameters, save generator presets, and select a suitable combination of effects with custom parameters.

Let's create a nice Software Instrument guitar:

1 Open the Instrument test song if it isn't already open.

2 Click the Genny Software Instrument track to bring up the Track Info window.

3 Click the Details triangle to access the generators and effects.

4 Click Guitars in the instrument category pane, as shown in Figure 8.32.

5 If it's not already selected, Select Guitar from the Generator pull-down menu.

6 Click the generator edit button to bring up the edit window. Select the Clean Electric Guitar preset from the preset pull-down menu.

7 Adjust the Release slider so that it is at a 50% level, as shown in Figure 8.33.

8 Select Make Preset from the preset pull-down menu. Name this preset `Electric Ring` and click Save.

FIGURE 8.32
Since we going to create a guitar, it's a good idea to be in the Guitars category.

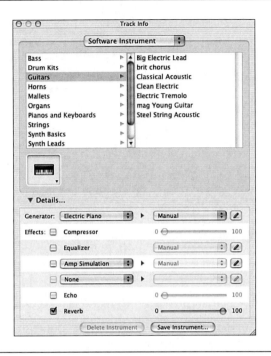

FIGURE 8.33
The preset menu switched to Manual when we adjusted the Release to 50%.

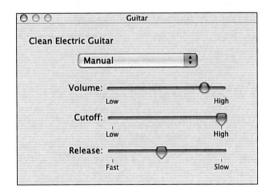

Congratulations, you've created a generator preset. Now let's add some effects:

1 Select Amp Simulation from the first assignable effect pull-down menu.

2 Select American Overdrive from the Effect preset pull-down menu, which gives us the amp sound that we want.

3 Select Tremolo from the second assignable effect pull-down menu.

4 Click the edit button to bring up the edit window if it isn't already up.

5 Adjust the sliders so that Intensity is 100% and Speed is at 75%; make sure the Auto Panning check box is checked, as shown in Figure 8.34.

FIGURE 8.34
Custom tremolo settings
are the only way to go.

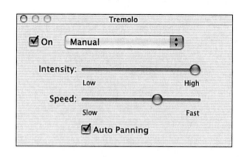

6 Select Make Preset from the preset pull-down menu. Name this preset `Medium Wide` and click Save.

7 Click the Echo check box to activate echo. Adjust the Echo slider to about 30%.

8 Click the Reverb check box to activate reverb. Adjust the Reverb slider to about 60%.

9 Click Save Instrument. Name the instrument `American Tremolo` and click Save to save our new Software Instrument.

Now that we've added a new guitar to your Software Instrument arsenal, you might want to open up the Keyboard window and play a little ditty with your new guitar instrument to take it out for a test drive. How about the "Star Spangled Banner," Hendrix-style?

We've noticed that GarageBand could use a few more vocal Real Instruments, particularly for backup vocals. Let's create a nice chorused vocal Real Instrument for backup vocals.

CREATING AND SAVING REAL INSTRUMENTS

Creating Real Instruments is even easier than creating Software Instruments since we don't have to deal with generators.

Let's create a vocal Real Instrument to add to your collection of Real Instruments:

1 Open the `Instrument test` song if it isn't already open.

2 Click the `No Effects` Real Instrument track to bring up the Track Info window.

3 Click the Details triangle to access the effects.

4 Click Vocals in the instrument category pane, and select Pop Vocals in the instrument list pane, as shown in Figure 8.35. We like the compressor and equalizer settings, so we'll leave them where they're at.

5 Select Chorus in place of Flanger in the first assignable effect slot.

6 Click the edit button to bring up the effects edit window. Adjust the Intensity slider to 100% and the Speed slider to about 15%, as shown in Figure 8.36.

FIGURE 8.35
Since we're going to create a vocal instrument, it's a good idea start with a vocal instrument.

FIGURE 8.36
Don't ya just love it when your intensity is at 100%?

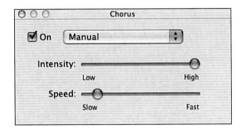

7 Select Make Preset from the preset pull-down menu. Name this preset **Doubler** and click Save.

8 Click the Echo check box to activate echo. Adjust the Echo slider to about 30%. Leave the Reverb slider at about 40%.

9 Click Save Instrument. Name the instrument **Double Chorus** and click Save to save your new Software Instrument.

Now you have a cool vocal Real Instrument for your bag of tricks. You can apply the effect to an existing vocal track or plug in a mic; dial up the new Double Chorus instrument; and sing, scat, rap, and scream to test it out. Now that you have created your own instruments, did you know that you could create your own Apple Loops too? That's exactly what we'll show you how to do in the next chapter.

MAKING YOUR OWN LOOPS

If you have 100 Apple Loops, you want 200. If you have 1,000, you want 2,000. That's just the way it is.

After you have bought Jam Pack and scoured the Web for free and commercial Apple Loops, you will want to know how to create your own audio loops and turn them into Apple Loops.

That's right, you can create Apple Loops from your own recordings and save them for use in your other songs or even share your loops with other GarageBand users for fun and profit.

And how about organizing and indexing your collection of Apple Loops? We'll show you how to keep your collection organized as well.

RECORDING YOUR OWN AUDIO LOOPS

The best way to avoid any licensing questions when your hit tune is up for a certain music award with a gramophone-shaped trophy in the Best Pop or Dance or R & B Song Created Using Loops but No Lip Sync category is to record your own loops.

CREATING AND SAVING AN AUDIO LOOP

Let's create and save an audio loop. This is the first step in the Apple Loop creation process:

1 Launch GarageBand and select File ┄┄⇥ New. Name your new song **Loop Test.**

2 For simplicity, let's create a four-measure synth lead in the key of C. Double-click the Grand Piano icon to bring up the Track Info window.

3 Select Synth Leads from the instrument category pane and Cheerful Trance from the instrument list pane. Then close the Track Info window.

4 Click Cycle to activate a cycle region. Drag to adjust the cycle region to cover the first four measures if it isn't there already, as shown in Figure 9.1.

FIGURE 9.1
"The cycle region now covers the first four bars," sounds like a sign in Sturgis, South Dakota.

tip
If you don't have a MIDI keyboard, you can use the Onscreen Musical Keyboard.

5 Activate both the Metronome and the Count-in in the Control menu.

6 Play a simple sequence of four whole notes going G, F, E, C in the middle octave of your keyboard.

7 Click the record button to record when you are ready. Click Play to exit recording and pause playback.

8 Click the track edit button to view your track, which should look like Figure 9.2.

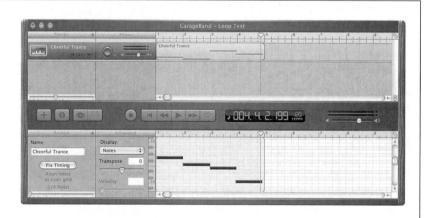

FIGURE 9.2
Wow! Four whole notes.

ADJUST THE NOTE TIMING

To ensure that our sequence loops well and to refresh some of our note editing skills, we'll shorten our notes to quarter notes:

1. Select each of the four notes in the edit grid. Then, drag the right side of each note of the sequence to the left to shorten it until it is a quarter note. Shorten all four notes until they are quarter notes, as shown in Figure 9.3.

2. Click Fix Timing to correct the timing of the notes so that each falls on the first beat of the measure.

3. Click Play to hear our sequence. The next step is to save our loop so that we can use it later.

> **note**
>
> If you want to know more about note editing and fixing note timing refer to Chapter 3, "Recording Your Own Music with Software Instruments."

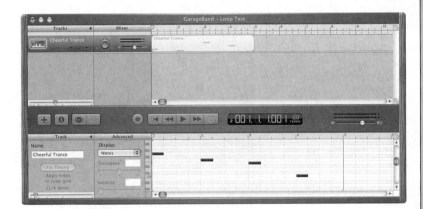

FIGURE 9.3
We're getting a refresher course in Software Instrument note editing.

4. Select File ⋯⟩ Export to iTunes. Also be sure to save the song at this point.

5. Now comes the hard part—finding the exported file. The exported file is saved by GarageBand in one of two places: If all is right with the world inside your Mac, you will find the file in the iTunes folder as *your name*, *your name*'s Album, Loop Test.aif. Otherwise, the file is the latest bounced file in your iTunes, Import folder.

   Once you find the file, drag the file onto the GarageBand timeline, where it will create a new Real Instrument track, as shown in Figure 9.4.

6. Click the Tempo indicator to bring up the Tempo slider. Drag the slider so the tempo is now 90 BPM. Notice that the imported audio track appears to have shortened in length compared to the Cheerful Trance Software Instrument track, as shown in Figure 9.5.

> **tip**
>
> If you can see your song in the iTunes Library, you can find the song file by Control-clicking the song name in iTunes. This pops up a contextual menu where you can select Show Song File to bring up a file menu showing the location of the song file on your hard drive.

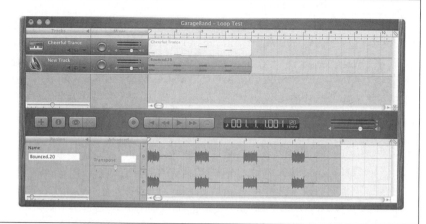

FIGURE 9.4
Our loop sequence is back, disguised as a Real Instrument region.

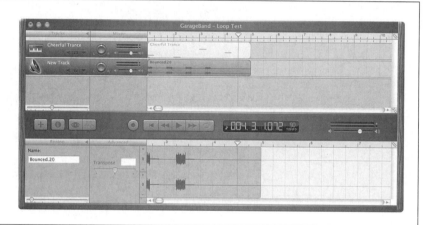

FIGURE 9.5
Uh oh, the tempo changed, but our imported audio loop didn't.

note

Imported audio loops are just Real Instrument regions and can be looped and manipulated like any other Real Instrument region. It is important to keep in mind, though, that imported audio loops don't have the ability to change key and tempo like Apple Loops do.

7 Go ahead and drag the Tempo slider back to 120 BPM; the loop is back to its proper length.

As long as you use an imported audio loop in a song in the same key and tempo as the original loop, you are okay.

CREATING A PSEUDO REAL INSTRUMENT APPLE LOOP

Before we get into changing our Real Instrument loop into a genuine Real Instrument Apple Loop, we'll show you how to create a pseudo-Apple Loop using a bit of trickery:

1 Duplicate our newly created Real Instrument loop by selecting Track ⸱⸱⸱⸱➔ New Basic Track. Option-drag the Real Instrument region that we created in the last section to the new track.

2 Position the playhead so that it is at measure 2 beat 1, as shown in Figure 9.6.

FIGURE 9.6
We are preparing to split the track at measure 2 beat 1.

3 Select Edit ····} Split.

4 Repeat the region splitting operation at measure 3 beat 1 and measure 4 beat 1. We now have four regions—one for each of our notes—as shown in Figure 9.7.

FIGURE 9.7
Now we have a region for every note of our sequence.

5 Click the Tempo indicator to bring up the Tempo slider. Drag the slider so the tempo is now 90 BPM. Notice that our cut-up track now expands to the same length as the Cheerful Trance Software Instrument track, as shown in Figure 9.8.

FIGURE 9.8
We tricked our way into being able to change the tempo.

6 Go ahead and drag the Tempo slider back to 120 BPM so that all the loops are back to their proper lengths.

As you can see, it is a very labor-intensive process to get a Real Instrument that you can change tempo with. If you are doing this with a drum loop or a denser piece of music, you will have to split the region into even smaller regions at all the notes or transitions in the region, not just at the start of each measure. But this is a good trick for creative effects or for sparse sounds if you need to change the tempo of a song.

As well as creating your own audio loops, there are hundreds of collections of audio loops, both commercial and freely available on the Web in a variety of audio formats. Better quality loop collections are sorted by tempo and key. You can import those loops as they are into GarageBand, and they will sound great as long as the tempo and key of the loop match the song's.

Of course, the best solution is to convert your audio loops into Apple Loops so that they can be used in songs at different tempos and keys.

CREATING APPLE LOOPS

Apple Loops are Apple's proprietary audio loop format that allows loops to adapt to the tempo and key of a song when used in Apple's GarageBand and SoundTrack products.

note

Apple Loops work with both GarageBand and Apple's SoundTrack program.

There are other proprietary loop formats out there that have the ability to adapt to different keys and tempos, such as Acid Loops and ReCycle Loops. But they are also limited to the programs that support them.

You can turn your audio loop collection into Apple Loops using Apple's free SoundTrack Loop Utility, which is part of the Apple Loops SDK and also included as a part of the SoundTrack application.

DOWNLOADING THE APPLE LOOPS SDK

To create your own Apple Loops, you will need to download the free Apple Loops SDK (Software Development Kit) from `http://developer.apple.com/sdk/#AppleLoops`. Click the Apple Loops SDK 1.1 SDK link to download the SDK.

tip

Five free Apple Loops are included as sample files with the Apple Loops SDK.

Once the package is downloaded, click the installer to install the contents.

If you don't have developer tools installed as part of your system, a Developer folder is created on your hard drive with an Apple Loops SDK folder in it. This folder contains the documentation and sample files for the SoundTrack Loop Utility. The actual utility is located in the `Applications/Utilities` folder.

USING THE SOUNDTRACK LOOP UTILITY

The SoundTrack Loop Utility is your ticket to creating your own Apple Loops for use in GarageBand.

In order to turn your plain-Jane audio file into being worthy of the Apple Loop label, the SoundTrack Loop Utility does two things:

- First, it automatically tries to mark the beats or transients in a sound file so that it can be stretched or shortened to work in different tempos and keys.
- Second, it saves a bunch of labels, called `tags`, with the file. These allow the file to be searched and browsed in GarageBand's Loop Browser.

Let's turn the audio loop that we created in the first section of this chapter into an Apple Loop:

1 Open the SoundTrack Loop Utility.

2 You are presented with a file open window that looks a little different with its serious gray color than a typical file open window (see Figure 9.9).

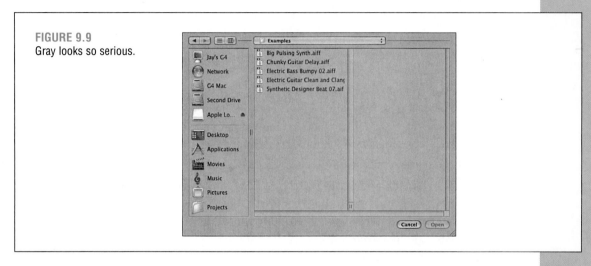

FIGURE 9.9
Gray looks so serious.

3 Go ahead and navigate to and open the audio loop file that we created in the first section of this chapter. Once this file is open, the SoundTrack Loop Utility looks like Figure 9.10.

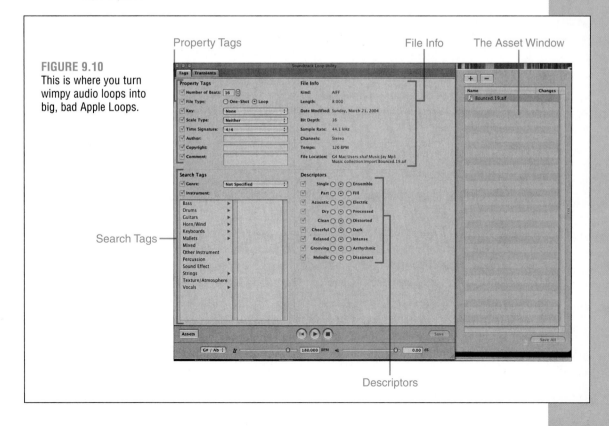

FIGURE 9.10
This is where you turn wimpy audio loops into big, bad Apple Loops.

Property Tags

File Info

The Asset Window

Search Tags

Descriptors

4 Click the play button in the bottom center of the window to hear our loop play back as a loop. Click the button again to stop playback.

Notice that the interface consists of two parts: the main window and the kind-of-hanging-off window called the Assets window.

Notice that the Assets window contains our audio loop file.

The main window is divided into four quadrants. The four quadrants are titled: Property Tags, File Info, Search Tags, and Descriptors.

The Property Tags allow you to save a number of tags with your files that are helpful to GarageBand's Loop Browser:

- **Number of Beats tag**—Allows you to set the length of the loop in beats. The utility generally does a good job of setting this property automatically. In our case, the loop is four measures long, which equates to 16 beats in 4/4 time.

- **File Type radio buttons**—Allow you to set whether your file is intended to loop or is a one-shot sound file. An example of a one-shot file might be a sound effect.

- **Key menu**—Allows you to set the musical key or root note of your file. In our case, the key of our file is C.

- **Scale Type menu**—Allows you to save whether the file is in a major or minor key. In our case, our file is in C major.

- **Time Signature menu**—Allows you to set the time signature of your file if it is other than 4/4 (common) time.

- **Author field**—Saves your name along with your creation.

- **Copyright field**—Lets you set your copyright information.

- **Comment field**—This is where you can thank the Academy.

In addition to the file's property tags, you can set search tags and descriptors for the file. These simply add the tags that classify your file for GarageBand's Loop Browser:

- **Genre tag**—This lets you set a genre for the file, so that the file is searchable by genre in GarageBand. In our case, the genre is electronic.

- **Instrument selector**—This allows you to set the Loop Browser categories for your file. In our sample file, we will select Keyboards ⋯⟩ Synthesizer.

The Descriptors radio buttons allow you to set the subjective qualities of your loop.

Clicking Save in the lower-right corner of the main window saves our loop file with all the tags that we have set, thus making the file officially an Apple Loop.

While this was technically all we needed to do to save our file as an Apple Loop, we would be remiss if we didn't point out a few more of the SoundTrack Loop Utility's features.

First is the ability to batch process files. Like a playlist in iTunes, you can add several files to the asset list in the Assets window.

note

The more tags you set for a loop, the easier it will be to find the file in GarageBand's Loop Browser.

You can add files to the list by dragging them onto the Assets window or by clicking the plus button in the upper-right corner of the Assets window, as shown in Figure 9.11.

To batch-process a list of files, you must choose at least the instrument tag for the files. Then you can click Save All in the lower-left corner of the Assets window.

However, if you batch-process your files, be aware that the SoundTrack Loop Utility is automatically applying property tags for the loops. Occasionally, the utility misinterprets the files and may, for example, think that an 80-BPM four-measure file is a 160-BPM two-measure file.

FIGURE 9.11
The Assets window is where you manage your loop files. ASSets, very funny, stop your giggling.

By individually processing your audio loops, you can check to see that the files are interpreted correctly and add more descriptive tags to the file.

In addition to the Assets window, the SoundTrack Loop Utility has the Transients window.

You can access the Transients window by clicking the Transients tab in the upper-left corner of the main window.

The Transients window is where the slicing and dicing goes on that allows the loop files to change tempo (see Figure 9.12).

FIGURE 9.12
The Transients window is where sound files are sliced, diced, and puréed, so that they can be stretched and shrunk to match tempo.

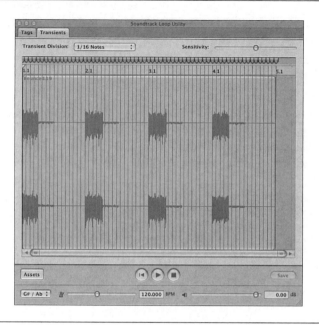

We don't want to mess around too much in the Transients window as the utility does its magic pretty much automatically.

If you look to the bottom of the window just below the playback controls and the Assets and Save buttons, you will notice a bar with a couple of sliders and a pull-down menu. This is the preview bar.

The preview bar allows you to listen to your files at different tempos, musical keys, and even volume levels. Note that these controls only affect the playback of your file and don't actually affect the file that you are saving.

Once you start processing a lot of loops, you may find you want to preview them in the Transients window at different keys and speeds. Sometimes notes may skip or tones may sound warbly if the divisions aren't set satisfactorily for your particular sequence.

Hopefully, we've given you a quick overview of how to use the SoundTrack Loop Utility. If you want to learn more on setting up markers in the Transients window and other features of the utility, take some time to read the documentation included with the download of the SDK. Next, let's find our newly created Apple Loop and import it into GarageBand.

IMPORTING YOUR APPLE LOOPS INTO GARAGEBAND

In order to make our Apple Loop available to GarageBand, we have to import it. We can just drag the file into GarageBand's Loop Browser window to import it and index it. However, GarageBand indexes the file at its current location on your hard drive under its current name, neither of which is desirable.

Let's rename our file and put it someplace where we can find it again.

Apple's Apple Loops are stored in the Library/Application Support/GarageBand/Apple Loops directory in a folder titled Apple Loops for Garage Band. Create a folder in the Apple Loops directory named `My Own Apple Loops` and possibly even another directory called `Third Party Apple Loops` if you are downloading any third-party Apple Loops from the Web. Find the Apple Loops file that we created with the SoundTrack Loop Utility. If all is right with the world inside your Mac, you will find the file in the iTunes folder called `your name, your name's Album, Loop Test.aif`. Otherwise, the file is the latest bounced file in your iTunes, Import folder.

Once you have found the file, move it into the `My Apple Loops` folder if you created one.

Rename the file to something more descriptive, such as **`Synth sequence 01.aif`**:

1. Launch GarageBand and open the `Loop Test` song. Click Loop Browser to open the Loop Browser.

2. Drag the entire `My Apple Loops` folder onto the Loop Browser window. A dialog pops up to tell you that GarageBand is indeed indexing your loops.

3. Click Synths and then click Electronic in the Loop Browser.

4. Scroll the Loop Browser window until you find `Synth sequence 01`. Drag the `Synth sequence 01` Apple Loop onto the timeline just below our last Real Instrument track.

5. Click the Tempo indicator to bring up the Tempo slider. Drag the slider so that the tempo is now 90 BPM.

Notice that the old imported audio track appears to have shortened in length compared to our newly added `Synth sequence 01` Apple Loop, sliced-up region and the original Cheerful Trance Software Instrument track (see Figure 9.13).

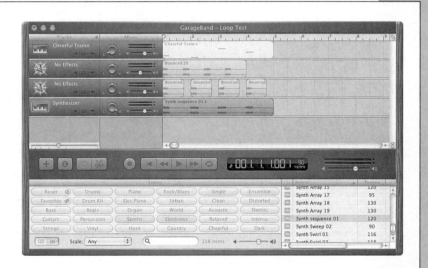

FIGURE 9.13
Our sample sequence is a bit lame, but now you can create your own way cooler Apple Loops.

caution

Shifting the song's tempo or key by large amounts will result in Apple Loops sounding unnatural when compared to their original keys or tempos.

note

Several free Apple Loops from Mac Audio Guy are available at http://macaudioguy.com/gbb/downloads/.

tip

Regularly drag your entire Apple Loops directory into the Loop Browser window to update your Apple Loops index.

You could adjust the tempo of the song and our sliced-up region would still fit. You can adjust the tempo or the key of the song or even transpose our new Apple Loop and it will still fit with the song.

Go ahead and save the `Loop Test` song. Next, we'll take a brief look at using third-party Apple Loops.

USING THIRD-PARTY APPLE LOOPS

There are hundreds, if not thousands, of free Apple Loops available on the Web already. When downloading and installing these Apple Loops, a little housekeeping on your Mac will help in keeping your loops organized and make managing your collection less of a headache.

INSTALLING THIRD-PARTY APPLE LOOPS

Remember that in the last section we said Apple's Apple Loops are stored in the `Library/Application Support/GarageBand/Apple Loops` directory in a folder titled `Apple Loops for Garage Band`.

We suggested at that point creating a folder named `Third Party Apple Loops`. The reason is that, as you expand your Apple Loop library, you will be able to sort between Apple's, third-party, and your own Apple Loops easily.

After you download Apple Loops from the Web, depending on how they are archived, either install or move the loops into your `Third Party Apple Loops` folder. And you'll be good to go.

INDEXING THIRD-PARTY APPLE LOOPS

It's easy to make sure that all your third-party Apple Loops are browsable and searchable in GarageBand's Loop Browser.

All you have to do is drag the `Third Party Apple Loops` folder onto the Loop Browser window to update your entire collection.

In the next chapter we're going to show you how to add and use third-party Audio Unit instruments and effects with GarageBand. We'll also introduce you to some advanced GarageBand and general recording tips and techniques.

ADVANCED TECHNIQUES

Y ou've learned how to record and save songs using Apple Loops, Software Instruments, and Real Instruments. But what about the really good stuff that they don't tell you about in the GarageBand documentation? Well, read on my friend because this chapter is GarageBand's X-Files.

USING AUDIO UNIT INSTRUMENTS AND EFFECTS

There is a saying in the audio industry: "We love standards, that's why we have so many of them." This saying has never been truer than when applied to audio plug-in formats.

As we mentioned in the previous chapter, Audio Units are Apple's own audio plug-in format. There are other plug-in formats out there from various manufacturers. By far, the most prevalent audio plug-in is the VST (Virtual Studio Technology) format, promoted by German software developer Steinberg.

When Apple acquired the Logic line of professional audio products, it decided that it needed its own plug-in format and came up with Audio Units, which are optimized for your Mac's OSX Core Audio Architecture.

Over the last year, developers have rushed to port over their VST instruments and effects and create new Audio Unit instruments and effects.

Enough of the history. First we'll tell you how to use Audio Unit (AU) instruments with GarageBand and then we'll go into AU effects in GarageBand.

AUDIO UNIT INSTRUMENTS FOR GARAGEBAND

We talked about Apple's DLSMusicDevice in Chapter 8, "Making Your Own Software and Real Instruments," which introduced you to Audio Unit instruments. Now let's take a look at a couple of third-party AU instruments.

Some examples of AU instruments are excellent commercial products like

- Native Instrument's $299 Absynth 2 (http://www.nativeinstruments.de/)
- BitHeadz's $499 Unity Session 3.3 (http://www.bitheadz.com/)

Or freeware bargains like these are available:

- Green Oak's Crystal (http://greenoak.com/). Note that the AU version of Crystal is on the VST downloads page.
- Ultimate Sound Bank's PlugSound Free (http://www.usbsounds.com/).

For the purposes of this book, let's take a look at Green Oak's Crystal. Crystal can be downloaded at http://greenoak.com/crystal/download.html.

Make sure that you download the AU version. Once the file has downloaded and unstuffed, you will have a file called `Crystal.component`. Move this file to your `Library/Audio/Plug-ins/Components` directory.

Next, let's launch GarageBand to check out our new instrument:

1 Create a new song and call it `AU Test`.

2 Double-click the Grand Piano icon to bring up the Track Info window.

3 Click the Details triangle in the lower-left corner of the Track Info window.

4 Scroll down the Generator pull-down menu and select Crystal, as shown in Figure 10.1.

note

Sources on the Web to find AU instruments include the Mac Music Web site (http://macmusic.org/softs/) and the Audio Units Web site (http://audiounits.com/).

caution

Audio Unit instruments are processor intensive. You need at least a G4 733MHz Mac to use AU instruments in GarageBand.

FIGURE 10.1
Aye, Captain, we've got to select the Crystal AU in the Generator menu or we won't have enough power!

5 Click the Generator edit button to bring up the Crystal edit window, as shown in Figure 10.2.

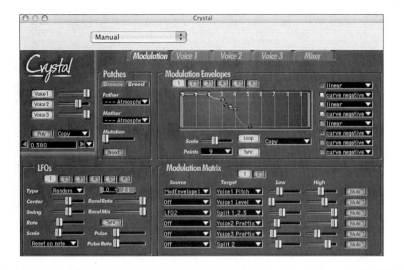

FIGURE 10.2
The Crystal interface doesn't exactly conform to Apple's Aqua interface look.

6 Select the preset pull-down menu in the upper-left corner of the Crystal interface right below the Poly and Copy buttons, as shown in Figure 10.3.

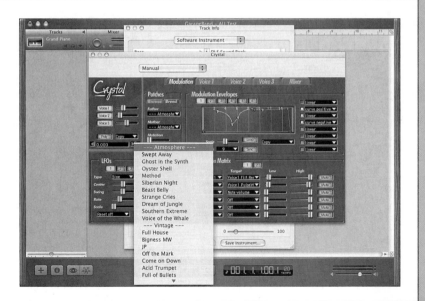

FIGURE 10.3
The preset menu is not easy to find, but there are 112 juicy synth presets hiding there.

7 Scroll down four slots in the Atmosphere section and select the Method preset from the preset menu. Go to the edit window preset pull-down menu at the top center of the window and select Make Preset. Name the preset `Crystal Method`, as shown in Figure 10.4.

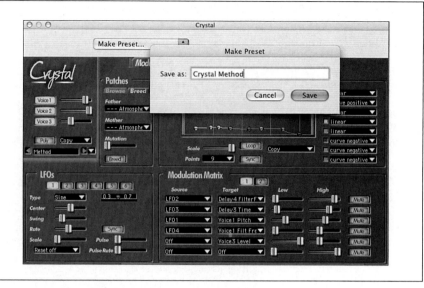

FIGURE 10.4
We are saving the Crystal Method preset for use in GarageBand.

8 Close the Crystal edit window.

9 Notice that you now have a Crystal Method preset for the Crystal Generator in the Track Info window (see Figure 10.5).

FIGURE 10.5
That's one brand-new Software Instrument; are you ready for the next 111?

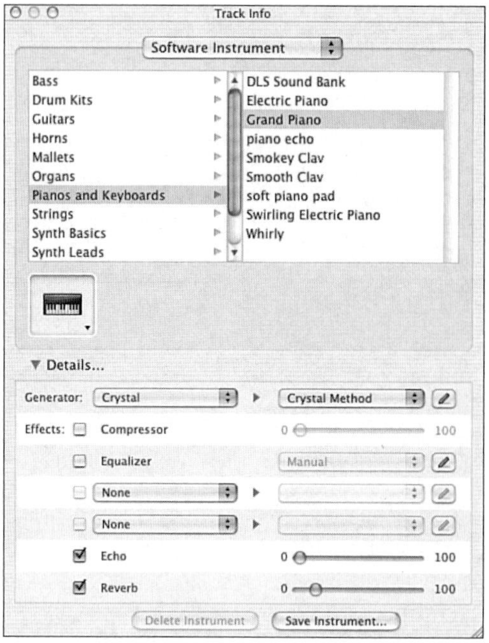

10 Select Synth Pads in the Track Info window Instrument category pane.

11 Click Save Instrument and name the instrument `Crystal Method`.

There you have it. We have just created a new Software Instrument for GarageBand using an AU instrument. You could go back and repeat this process 111 times to have all of Crystal's presets available to GarageBand or, more likely, you can save out a preset from the Crystal preset list for use in GarageBand whenever you need it in a particular song.

You can also edit or create presets for Crystal using Crystal's own interface within the Generator edit window.

With Audio Unit instruments added to GarageBand's already powerful built-in generators, the possibilities for sound creation are virtually limitless. Next, let's look at AU effects.

AUDIO UNIT EFFECTS FOR GARAGEBAND

Audio Unit instruments are great, but Audio Unit effects are even better because they don't suck up as much processor power and can be used with Real Instruments as well as with Software Instruments.

Sources on the Web to find AU effects include the Mac Music Web site (`http://macmusic.org/softs/`) and the Audio Units Web site (`http://www.audiounits.com/`).

Some examples of AU effects are excellent and expensive commercial products like these:

- Cycling 74's $199 Pluggo Bundle (`http://www.cycling74.com/products/pluggo.html`)
- Metric Halo's $349 Channel Strip (`http://www.mhlabs.com/`)

Or, freeware bargains like these are available:

- MDA effects (`http://mda-vst.com/`)
- Super Destroy FX (`http://destrofx.smartelectronix.com`)

When you download or buy AU effects, make sure that you get the AU version. Also be sure to put AU effects into your `Library/Audio/Plug-ins/Components` directory.

It's really easy for your effects collection to grow in a hurry (see Figure 10.6).

The important thing to remember is to explore your effects to see what each one does. That will tell you when to use a particular effect or maybe even when not to use any effects at all.

Now that you are loaded with knowledge to create enough Apple Loops, Software Instruments, and effects to keep you busy for a couple of years, let's look at some of GarageBand's not-so-obvious features.

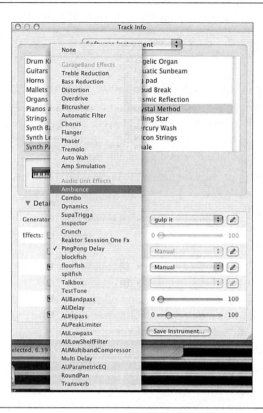

FIGURE 10.6
Twenty-four Audio Unit effects and counting.

GARAGEBAND TIPS AND TRICKS

One of GarageBand's minor faults is that some of its most powerful features are undocumented and therefore ignored or, worst yet, dissed by people who don't know that these features exist. In this section we'll show some really awesome and relatively unknown things that you can do with GarageBand.

THE IMPORTING MIDI FILES TRICK

Many musicians or music enthusiasts out there have MIDI files in their collections and would love to see how they could benefit from GarageBand's Software Instruments. If nothing else, it'd be cool to import MIDI files and sing over them karaoke style.

Thankfully, there is a freeware utility out there that will let you import your MIDI files into GarageBand. It's called Dent Du MIDI by Bery Rinaldo and is available for download at `http://homepage.mac.com/beryrinaldo/ddm`. The name of the program, Dent Du MIDI, is the name of a mountain in the Swiss Alps, which is pronounced *don't do MIDI*. Clever, huh? But not as clever as the program.

Dent Du MIDI is a simple droplet-type application with a few conversion options and a MIDI drum remapper (see Figure 10.7).

FIGURE 10.7
Just drop the MIDI file and step away from the application.

Dent Du MIDI's conversion options are

- **Pass Through Program Change Events**—While GarageBand itself doesn't recognize these messages, the DLSMusicDevice does. Check this if you plan to use the device. This option is defaulted to Off because program change events have been known to hang GarageBand.

- **Pass Through Volume Change Events**—Volume changes in the MIDI file show up in GarageBand as the track's volume curve. This option is defaulted to On.

- **Pass Through Pan Change Events**—Although GarageBand doesn't display pan automation, setting this option to On preserves the MIDI file's pan information. The default is On.

- **Translate Drum Tracks**—This option allows you to remap nonstandard MIDI drum tracks to GarageBand's standard drum map. The default is Off.

- **Add Track Name from MIDI File**—If your MIDI file has track names, this option is really handy to help you keep track of the proper instruments. The default is On.

- **Add General MIDI Program Name**—If you are importing a general MIDI file, this option tries to assign instrument names to the tracks. The default is Off.

- **Output MIDI Files**—This option should only be used to break a MIDI file into individual MIDI track files. The output files cannot be imported into GarageBand. The default is Off.

To convert a MIDI file or files, just drop them onto the mountain icon. A progress bar tells you when the conversion is complete. Dent Du MIDI creates a folder with the original MIDI filename in the original directory with -GB appended to it. Inside the folder is an .aif file for each of the MIDI tracks in the MIDI file.

To import the files into GarageBand, follow these steps:

note

A sample MIDI file titled KOOLIT.MID and the converted GarageBand song file MIDI Test are available at http://macaudioguy/gbb/downloads/.

1 Launch GarageBand and create a new song.

2 Delete the Grand Piano track.

3 Drag the converted .aif files onto GarageBand's timeline. All the files appear as tracks in GarageBand.

4 Assign a Software Instrument to each track.

An example of a converted MIDI file is shown in Figure 10.8.

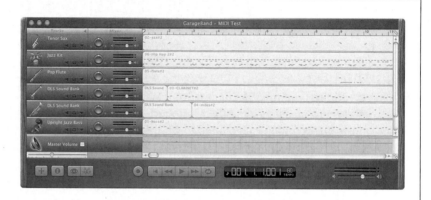

FIGURE 10.8
Living proof that GarageBand does do MIDI.

THE REWIRE TRICK

This one is pretty obscure for most GarageBand users, but it's so good we couldn't leave it out.

ReWire is a proprietary standard that allows different sound programs to synchronize with one another, where one program is the master and the other program is the slave. The master program's transport buttons, like Play and Stop, control the slave as well. Other settings like tempo are shared between the two programs.

Programs such as Logic, Cubase, Pro Tools, and Reason all support ReWire either as a master or slave. The secret is that GarageBand can act as a ReWire master.

This means that you can run GarageBand and control a program that runs as a ReWire slave, such as Reason and Abelton Live.

Reason is a $499 virtual studio application from Propellerhead Software. Reason has excellent MIDI and Software Instrument capabilities but can't record Real Instruments. Adding GarageBand's Real Instrument recording capabilities to Reason is a match made in audio heaven.

All you need to do to get ReWire to work is to launch GarageBand first and then launch the ReWire slave application.

Once the ReWire connection is automatically established, you will be able to control the slave app with GarageBand and the slave app's audio output will be mixed with GarageBand's output. You can even export the mix to iTunes, and the resulting song will have both GarageBand's and the slave app's tracks.

Figure 10.9 shows GarageBand and Reason running together.

FIGURE 10.9
GarageBand is the master of its ReWire slave, Reason.

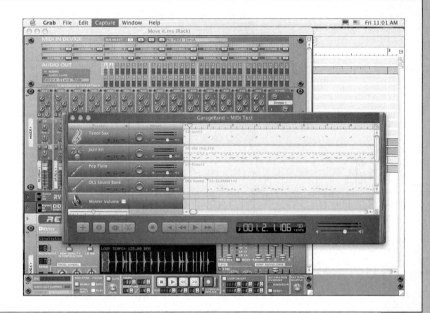

THE SOUNDFLOWER TRICK

This next trick is one that you have to be pretty creative to figure out how it can be useful. But it is quite useful and doesn't cost a thing.

Soundflower is a virtual audio driver and is a free download from Cycling 74 at `http://www.cycling74.com/`.

Soundflower's usefulness lies in its ability to route the audio output of one application or device to another application or device.

What use is this for GarageBand? Recording the audio output of another sound program directly into GarageBand without first having to record a file that GarageBand can import is both a time-saver and a disk space saver.

Another use might be to record sound from a FireWire camcorder or other FireWire device into GarageBand.

Or, how about recording an Internet radio broadcast? Or, how about recording your GarageBand song to another audio program without exporting to iTunes?

Like we said, Soundflower can be quite useful.

We'll show you how to record an Internet radio broadcast into GarageBand:

1 Download and install the Soundflower driver.

2 Launch iTunes, select an Internet radio station, and begin playing the station (see Figure 10.10).

FIGURE 10.10
Old school techno is our cup of tea; you can listen to whatever you what.

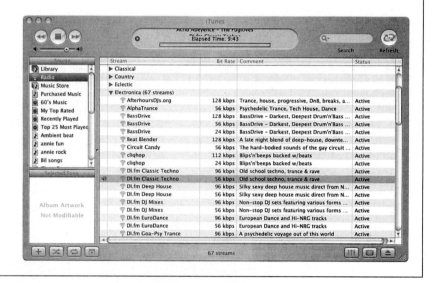

3 Launch GarageBand, open a new song, and call it `Rip Test`. Delete the Grand Piano track.

4 Select GarageBand ┈┈▷ Preferences. Select the Audio/MIDI tab.

5 Select Soundflower (2Ch) from the Audio Input pull-down menu, as shown in Figure 10.11.

FIGURE 10.11
Selecting Soundflower as an audio input probably won't hurt your allergies.

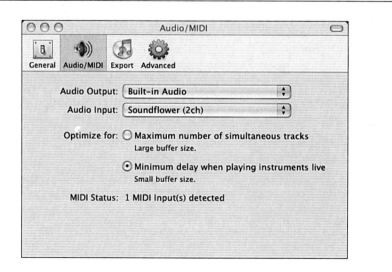

6 Select System Preferences from the Apple menu in the Finder. Select Sound preference, and then click the Output tab.

7 Select Soundflower (2ch) from the output menu, as shown in Figure 10.12. Close the System Preferences window.

FIGURE 10.12
A Soundflower by any other name is still an output driver.

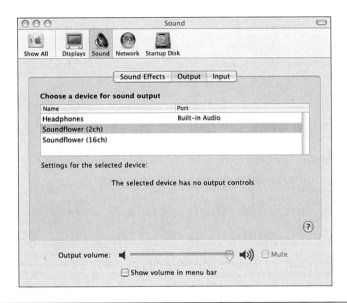

8 In GarageBand, create a new Real Instrument track. Select Basic Track ⸱⸱⸱⸱▸ No Effects and click the Monitor radio button to On. Click OK.

9 Click the record button to begin recording the Internet radio broadcast, as shown in Figure 10.13.

FIGURE 10.13
Why you would want to record an Internet radio broadcast is left to your own imagination.

After using Soundflower to route audio, it's a good idea to return to your default audio input and output settings both in the Finder System Preferences and in GarageBand's Preferences.

Having Soundflower on your Mac is like having a Swiss army knife in your pocket—you never know exactly when you'll need it or for what, but it's sure nice to know that it's there.

THE "GARAGEBAND AS A DIGITAL RECORDER" TRICK

It should be obvious that GarageBand is a great stereo audio recorder. And it can even act as an audio editor. But you'd be surprised how many people overlook this capability.

We have heard that GarageBand could only record 1 hour of audio. We did our own experiment and found that this is not true. You can record as long as your hard drive will let you (see Figure 10.14).

FIGURE 10.14
The counter is past 1 hour and GarageBand is still chewing up our hard drive.

note

A GarageBand stereo Real Instrument track uses about 10MB of disk space for every minute of recording.

Let's say that you needed to record several half-hour presentations during a conference. One way to record them would be to create a new song for each session; another would be to create a new track for each session.

Now here comes the good part—you don't have to export your recording to iTunes. Locate your song project, which is usually in the GarageBand folder inside of your Music folder in your user directory. All you have to do is Control-click the song file to bring up its contextual menu and select Show Package Contents, as shown in Figure 10.15.

FIGURE 10.15
Selecting Show Package Contents is like opening a present.

Help

Open
Open With ▶
Get Info

Color Label:
✕ ⬤ ◯ ◯ ◯ ◯ ◯ ◯

Show Package Contents
Move to Trash

Duplicate
Make Alias
Create Archive of "MIDI Test"

Copy "MIDI Test"

Toast It
Enable Folder Actions
Configure Folder Actions...

In the song file contents window there are two folders, the `ProjectData` file that contains the Software Instrument and effects settings for the song and the `Media` folder that contains the Real Instrument tracks for the song.

Open the `Media` folder and you will see your Real Instrument tracks as, guess what, `.aif` audio files (see Figure 10.16).

FIGURE 10.16
So, this is where they hide the audio files.

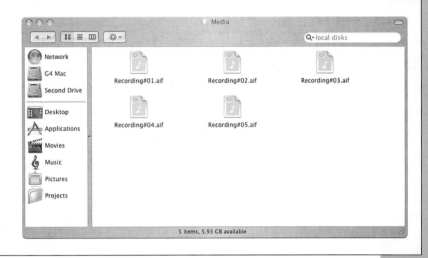

You can copy these files directly to another audio editor, your CD burning software, or even import them to iTunes.

THE GREAT RECOVERY TRICK

This trick allows you to recover a deleted track if, and only if, you have not saved your song file since deleting the track.

If you suddenly realize that you really liked that first-take vocal track that you deleted five tracks ago and wished you could get it back, we have a trick for you. If you have not saved your song file, you can open the song file by selecting Show Package Contents like in the previous trick and then dragging the lowest-numbered recording files back into GarageBand. And if you are lucky, your first take will be among the recovered tracks.

⚠ caution

Regardless of this trick, we still recommend that you save your song file often.

RECORDING TRICKS AND TECHNIQUES

In this next section we'll look at a few universal recording tricks that work with GarageBand as well as other recording software.

BOUNCING TRACKS

Bouncing is an old recording term that refers to a method used to get seven tracks of audio on a four-track analog tape recorder. The technique involves mixing three tracks onto track 4. Then, you erase tracks 1, 2, and 3 and record on tracks 1 and 2. Next, you mix them to track 3, erase tracks 1 and 2, and record on them again. This was working without a net, to say the least. Thankfully, the days of such destructive processes have passed.

But a derivative of this old trick can get you more tracks to record with in GarageBand.

As we have explained throughout this book, Software Instruments eat up processor power like Anna Nicole eats bonbons. Real Instrument tracks are far less taxing on your Mac's processor but are hell on your hard drive. If your Mac is threatening to puke out on you after your third Software Instrument track, here is what you can do:

1 Set up a mix that you like of the Software Instrument tracks.

2 Select File Export to iTunes.

3 Save your song to preserve your original instrument settings, and then open a new song.

4 Drag your mixed audio file from iTunes into your new song's timeline, where it becomes a Real Instrument track.

5 Continue recording Software or Real Instrument tracks until you've recorded your song or your Mac starts to croak again. And then bounce again if necessary.

Bouncing isn't pretty, but it can gain you more tracks. The advantage of this method is that, when you get a faster computer, you can go back and reconstruct all the tracks from the bounced songs.

If you wanted to get real fancy with this technique, you could even export the repetitive sections of your Software Instrument tracks, process them through the SoundTrack Loop Utility, and reimport them as Apple Loops.

tip

Exporting a Software Instrument track to iTunes and then reimporting the track as a Real Instrument track conserves your Mac's processor power and allows you to get more tracks out of GarageBand.

THE CROSS-FADE PAN TRICK

One recurrent complaint about GarageBand is that you cannot automate your pan settings the same way that you can your volume curves. We'll show how to automate your panning, and it will only cost you an extra Real Instrument track:

1 Launch Garage Band, open a new song, and name it `Pan Test`.

2 Delete the Grand Piano track.

3 Click Loop Browser and click Drums.

4 Select `Club Dance Beat 001` from the Loop Browser and drag it into the timeline.

5 Drag another copy of `Club Dance Beat 001` into the timeline to create a second track, as shown in Figure 10.17.

6 Click Cycle to create a cycle region over the two tracks.

7 Click the show track volume triangles for both tracks. Click to activate both Track volume check boxes.

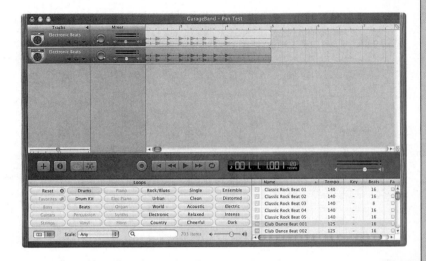

FIGURE 10.17
Two identical drum tracks are better than one.

8 Drag the first track's pan knob all the way to the left. Drag the second track's pan knob all the way to the right.

9 Create three control points in the first track's volume curve and drag them into the positions shown in Figure 10.18.

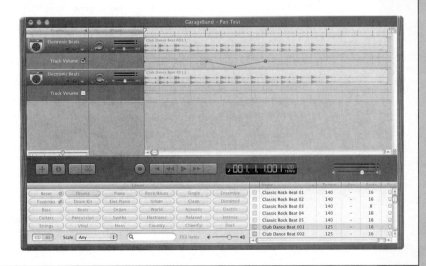

FIGURE 10.18
Fading out the left track pans the sound to the right.

10 Create three control points in the second track's volume curve and drag them into the positions shown in Figure 10.19.

As you can hear and see, by using clever fades we can pan the sound to the right and then the left and then back to the center. Who said we couldn't automate panning in GarageBand?

FIGURE 10.19
Houston, we have an automated pan.

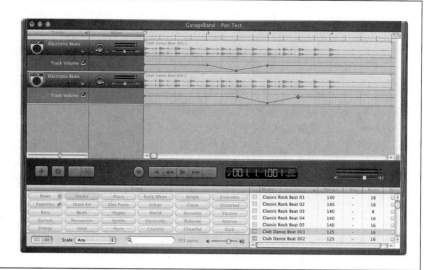

THE SPLITTING DRUMS TRICK

When recording albums, probably more time and effort are spent getting the drum sound than anything else. Typically, producers use up to 10 tracks just to record a drum kit and spend several hours to get just the right mic placements and effect settings for the kit.

With GarageBand, drum loops are either stereo Real Instrument loops with all of the drums mixed to two tracks or Software Instrument loops which may not even have any pan information at all recorded as part of the loop.

To get that big studio sound, you need to split out your drums to different tracks so that you can tailor your effects to each part of the kit to make a better sounding whole.

For stereo-mixed Real Instrument drums, this is a difficult operation where you must duplicate the track several times over and try to isolate the individual drums using equalizers. Not fun, and often not worth the effort.

However, Software Instrument drum loops do present us with the opportunity to individualize our drums.

Let's split up a Software Instrument drum loop:

1 Launch Garage Band, open a new song, and name it `Drum Test`.

2 Delete the Grand Piano track.

3 Click Loop Browser and click Drums.

4 Select `Classic Rock Beat 03` from the Loop Browser and drag it into the timeline.

5 Drag three copies of `Classic Rock Beat 03` into the timeline to create four tracks, as shown in Figure 10.20.

FIGURE 10.20
Now that's a stack of drum loops.

6 Click Cycle to create a cycle region over the loops.

7 Select the first track and click Edit to bring up the track editor.

8 Drag-select all the notes except the kick drum (C1) notes, as shown in Figure 10.21. Delete the selected notes.

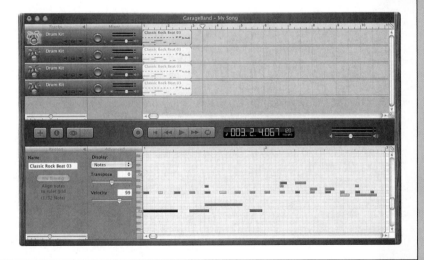

FIGURE 10.21
All the selected notes are going bye-bye.

9 Select the second track. Select and delete all of the notes except for the snare drum (D1).

10 Select the third track. Select and delete the kick drum (C1), snare drum (D1), and low tom-tom (F1) notes.

11 Select the fourth track. Select and delete the kick drum (C1), snare drum (D1), and high tom-tom (A1) notes.

12 Pan track 2 to about 2 o'clock, pan track 3 all the way to the right, and pan track 4 all the way to the left.

If you listen to the loop now, you'll notice that we've greatly increased the stereo effect of the drum kit. Next, name the track regions `Kick`, `Snare`, `OH right`, and `OH left` (see Figure 10.22). OH is recording jargon for overhead.

FIGURE 10.22
All the drums are getting their own tracks, effects, and pan settings. Aren't they special?

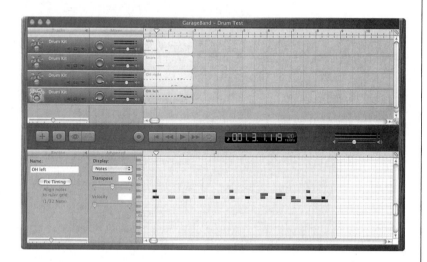

You can create a fifth track with the original `Classic Rock Beat 03` as a reference. That way, you can solo just this track to hear the original and then mute it to hear the newly split version.

By splitting the drum track, not only can we increase the stereo spread of the drum kit, but we can also give each track its own effects and level or even instrument settings. Download the `Drum Test` file from `http://macaudioguy.com/gbb/downloads/` to check out the effect settings that we chose.

Once you have a drum sound that you like, if your Mac has enough horsepower, you can keep the separate Software Instrument tracks as part of your song. Or, if your Mac isn't as powerful, you can export the drum tracks, process them through the SoundTrack Loop Utility, and reimport them as Apple Loops.

MORE DIVIDE-AND-CONQUER TRICKS

Duplicating tracks can open up all kinds of creative possibilities for your songs.

Here are a few tricks from up our sleeves:

- Duplicate a clean guitar track and then put some serious amp effects on the duplicated track. Then set up a very slow cross-fade between the two tracks. Instant automated effects.

- Duplicate a guitar track twice. Then pan one of the duplicated guitar tracks hard left and lower its volume; then move or *slip* the track so that it is delayed exactly 1/32 note in the timeline. Pan the other duplicated guitar track hard right and lower its volume; then move or *slip* the track so that it is delayed exactly 1/16 note in the timeline. Whoa! Talk about surround effects.

- Split the first note from a region and then duplicate it several times before the original note. Slowly fade up the duplicated notes for that backward echo effect.
- Duplicate a track, pan it opposite of the original track, and try radically different effects or even instruments for each.
- Duplicate a Software Instrument drum loop and switch it to a different Software Instrument drum kit. Pop Kit plus Hip Hop kit equals Hip Pop kit.

THE DOUBLED VOCALS TRICK

It is a rare hit pop song where the vocals aren't doubled at least in the chorus section of the song. There is a good reason for this—singing the part several times irons out any inconsistencies and gives the song more punch.

Merely duplicating a recorded track won't work in this case. If you are the singer, insist on recording at least two tracks of any vocal part. If you are a recordist, recording as many vocal takes as possible only makes sense.

Also sing the chorus part in harmony if you are able. It is very satisfying to sing harmony with yourself.

To create a harmony part with the SoundTrack Loop Utility, all you have to do is solo and export the part that you want to harmonize. Process the part through the SoundTrack Loop Utility and reimport the part as an Apple Loop. Finally, transpose the part in the track editor. Figure 10.23 shows a harmonized loop.

tip

If you can't sing harmony, you can use GarageBand and the SoundTrack Loop Utility to help.

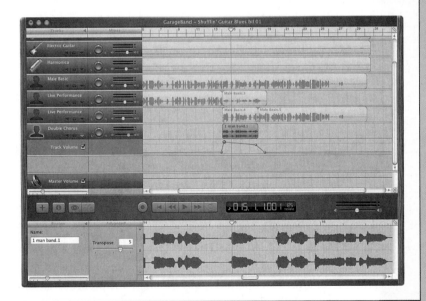

FIGURE 10.23
Maybe we can teach the world to sing in perfect harmony.

The harmonized loop may have a slightly metallic sound, but it will be in perfect harmony with your original track. A little equalization and some subtle effects and people will think you sang the harmony part perfectly.

FINAL TIPS FOR SPICING UP THE MIX

Here are some tips to help spice up your songs and mixes:

- Thicken up a weak vocal with the chorus effect.
- Make a bass sound punchier by boosting the upper mid frequencies with the Equalizer.
- Quiet a humming guitar amp with the gate effect.
- Have some friends over for cocktails and trick them into recording some background vocal tracks.
- Listen to your mixes on as many different speaker systems as possible. Especially listen to your mix on a car stereo or two.
- Unplug your home phone and turn off your cell phone when recording.
- The compressor effect works best on bass and vocals.
- A Real Instrument is always better than a Software Instrument for a lead part.
- It's easier to ruin a mix with too many effects than with too few.
- Additional percussion instruments can often be found in the kitchen.
- Really crazy ideas either succeed gloriously or fail miserably.
- Don't fool yourself—making a sound louder in the mix doesn't make it sound better.
- Steal from the best; listen closely to and copy techniques from albums that you like.
- Export several mixes of your song. Being able to pick and choose after your ears have healed is priceless.
- Everyone wants to hear more of themselves in a mix. Simply remind them that you have a Delete key and know how to use it.
- The cops usually come later if you close the garage door when playing.

WENDY CARLOS'S RECORDING TIPS FOR BEGINNERS

To reach synth goddess Wendy Carlos's humorous "Recording Tips for Beginners," go to http://www.apocalypse.org/~wendy/resources/studiotips.html.

FINAL THOUGHTS

Some in the recording industry have characterized GarageBand as a toy. It is not and we have hopefully shown that you can achieve professional results with GarageBand.

Others in the recording biz have seen it as taking business away from the recording studios. This may be partially true, but any empowering technology is going to bring fresh ideas to how music is recorded and have an overall positive effect.

Some are frustrated by its simplicity, others by its complexity. GarageBand can't be everything to everybody, but it comes very close at least for its market. And it attempts, at least, to be a product that doesn't get in the way of creativity.

What people forget is that great albums have been produced with technology that isn't even close to GarageBand's capabilities or its audio quality. Speaking personally as a recording engineer, I can do some things with GarageBand today than I couldn't have done with a quarter-million dollars' worth of studio gear 20 years ago. A reel of 1/4'' reel-to-reel tape used to cost the same as what you pay for GarageBand today.

As your interest and experience grow, you may want to move on to more expensive professional recording software—or you may not.

We look forward to the day when your garage band uses GarageBand to record the demo that gets you that mega record deal. Or better yet, the day when your garage band announces at the big awards show with the gramophone-shaped trophy that you recorded your big hit using GarageBand, a Mac in your basement...and this book.

GLOSSARY

A

amplifier   An electronic device that raises an audio signal level, resulting in a louder sound level.

amplitude   The absolute height of an audio signal waveform, which defines the loudness of a sound.

analog   An electrical waveform signal that is analogous to the sound pressure level waves in the air.

audio   Sound, but usually applied to the electrical or digital signal that represents sound.

audio input   The connection going into a computer or an audio device.

axe   Slang for instrument, usually a handheld instrument like a guitar or trumpet.

B

ballad   Usually a slower-tempoed song with voice as the primary instrument.

backbeat   Usually beats 2 and 4 of a measure in popular music.

bar   Measure. Also where bands play.

bass   Low-pitched range of sound. Also a low-pitched instrument such as a bass guitar or an upright double bass.

bass player   Musician who can be replaced by a pianist's left hand.

beat   A unit of musical time; a subdivision of a measure. The pulse of a song.

bpm   Beats per minute. Relates musical time to conventional time and defines the tempo.

C

chord   The sounding of two or more simultaneous notes.

chorus   A refrain or repeated portion of a song where repeated words are sung over a repeated melody. Also, an effect where the processed audio signal moves slightly out of time and tune with the original signal, creating the illusion of several instruments or singers.

clipping   When a signal exceeds a circuit's capacity to handle it, causing the signal to be truncated and resulting in a distorted sound.

compressor   An effect that reduces the overall volume range from the softest to the loudest by boosting lower volume and lessening higher volume parts of a signal.

cycle   GarageBand's term for looping a portion of a song.

D

decibel   Unit of sound volume measurement.

digital audio   An encoding and decoding scheme where an analog audio signal is represented as a string of binary numbers.

distortion   A harsh sound created by overloading an electrical circuit.

downbeat   The first beat of a measure.

drummer   A person who hangs out with musicians in a band.

dynamic range   The difference between the softest and the loudest part of a sound.

E

echo   An effect where a sound is delayed in time and repeated, usually at a lower volume.

effect   A process that changes the character of a sound.

equalizer   An effect that affects the frequency content of a sound.

F

fader   A linear or sliding volume control.

fifth   A pleasing musical interval seven semitones or five notes above the tonic note. An example is G above C. When the band can't afford a quart.

flanger   An effect where the processed audio signal moves slowly in and out of time with the original signal.

flat   A note which is lowered one-half step in pitch. A place for British musicians to crash.

frequency   The cyclic variation of an audio signal in cycles per second or hertz (Hz). The hearing range of humans is usually said to be between 20Hz and 20,000Hz. It's often used to describe the pitch range of a sound. An example would be an equalizer can boost low frequencies.

G

gain   Measurement of signal amplification. Another term for volume level.

guitarist   A music critic armed with a guitar.

H - I

harmonics The overtones of a sound which happen at musical intervals or whole number multiples of a sound.

harmony A pleasing combination of notes sounded together. Usually an interval of third or fifth for vocals.

hertz (Hz) The measure of pitch of a sound. 1Hz equals one cycle per second of a sound's waveform.

hum Low-frequency interference to an audio signal, usually at 60Hz, caused by power source interference.

interval The distance between two pitches.

K

key A pleasing-to-the-ear series of eight musical notes that begins and ends with the root or starting note. Also a physical part of an instrument, i.e. piano keys.

kick drum The bass drum of a drum kit.

kilohertz 1,000Hz or cycles per second.

L

lead singer Person in the band who doesn't mind standing around holding a tambourine.

lyrics The words of a song.

M - N

major key A musical scale generally thought to have a happy sound.

measure A unit of musical time made up of beats and defined by the time signature, also called a *bar*.

melody The series of notes that form the musical shape of a song. The hummable part of a song.

metronome A device that keeps musical time.

middle C Note that has a pitch of 261.63Hz. Generally found at the middle of a piano keyboard.

MIDI (Musical Instrument Digital Interface) A computer language for transmitting and storing musical information.

minor key A musical scale generally thought to have a sadder sound.

mixer A device that combines audio signals.

monitors A pair of loudspeakers.

mono A single channel audio signal.

musician Musical performer who is usually employed in the food service industry.

mute A control that silences a particular track.

note A single musical tone.

O

octave A tone range of 12 semitones in which the pitch of a note is doubled.

overdub To record on an unused track while listening to previously recorded tracks.

P

pan   The panoramic illusion of a sound's placement in space from left to right.

patch   A collection of sound generator or effects parameters; also called a *preset*.

percussion instruments   Instruments that are generally struck to make sound.

phaser   An effect where the processed audio signal is slightly out of phase or time with the original signal.

pitch   The discrete frequency of a sound where a low-frequency sound is perceived as a low-pitched note and a high-frequency sound is perceived as a high-pitched note.

preset   A stored set of parameters.

punch-in   Recording onto a portion of a previously recorded track. In GarageBand, this refers to region recording.

Q - R

quarter note   A note having the duration of 1/4 of a whole note, which is usually one measure in duration.

Real Instrument   GarageBand's term for an effect preset for sound that is either input or imported into GarageBand.

region   In GarageBand, a unit of recorded sound or MIDI information.

reverb   An effect that seeks to emulate the reflections of sound in space. An example would be that a shower stall is a small reverberant space.

root note   Usually the beginning note for a scale. The fundamental or defining note for a key or a chord.

S

scale   A repeating series of (usually 8) discrete pitches.

semitone   The smallest pitch division of a scale.

sharp   A note that is raised one semitone in pitch.

Software Instrument   A term used by GarageBand to define an instrument preset that includes an internal sound generator as well as effects.

solo   A control which allows you to hear a specific track exclusively. Also a portion of a song where one instrument is allowed to predominate.

song   A musical composition. Also in GarageBand, the project file where all the software settings and performance information are stored.

sound   Rapid variations of fluid (air, water, and so on) pressure that can be detected by the ear.

stereo   Two channels of audio recorded simultaneously in near proximity so as to create an illusion of 3D space when reproduced.

synthesizer   An electronic musical instrument which combines sound generators and modifiers that can be controlled.

T

tempo   The relationship between real time and musical time expressed in beats per minute.

third   Musical interval spanning four semitones. An example is C to E.

timbre   The character of a sound. For example, a piano and a guitar sound different even when playing the same note.

timing   The relationship between musical events and musical time. It is usually desirable to have a musical event happen on the musical beat or a subdivision of the beat.

tone   In music theory, a musical interval of two semitones. Also the harmonic quality of a sound. For example, a flute has a pure tone, whereas a cello has a complex or dark tone.

track   In GarageBand, it's either a mono or stereo audio or MIDI data channel. Multitrack recording is where several tracks of data are overlaid.

transpose   To move a note or series of notes up or down in pitch.

tremolo   Slight up and down variation of the volume of the sound of a note.

tuning   The referencing of an instrument to a specific frequency. Also adjusting instruments so that they are playing at the same frequency as other instruments.

U - Z

unison   Two or more instruments playing the same notes.

velocity   How quickly or hard a keyboard key is struck, which usually defines the volume of a note.

verse   The exposition part of a song where different words are sung to a repeating melody.

vibrato   Slight rapid up and down variation of the pitch of a note.

volume   A measurement of the loudness of a sound.

waveform   A graphical representation of a sound or audio signal.

whole note   Usually a note duration of one measure.

EXPANDING GARAGEBAND

I
f you are having fun with GarageBand, you may find it worthwhile to expand its capabilities. You can do that with the GarageBand Jam Pack and some third-party products.

You can never have enough RAM, and soon you will find the same is true of Apple Loops. Once you have tired of the almost 2000 loops and 50+ software instruments that come with GarageBand, you will want more, more, more!

THE GARAGEBAND JAM PACK

Apple has just the thing for that uncontrollable desire for more and more sounds to feed your GarageBand habit. And it will only cost you twice as much as the original program.

Why should you spend $99 to expand a $49 product, you ask. Because it is worth every penny. For only $99, you can add over 2,000 more Apple Loops, over 100 more Software Instruments, 100 more effects settings, and 15 more guitar amp settings. Having that many sounds to choose from should scratch the itch and keep you off the street for a little while.

Beyond the price tag, having all that selection does have its downside. And that downside is disk space. Add another 3GB to the 2.5GB that GarageBand is already occupying, and 5.5GB of disk space for one pro-gram plus all of your GarageBand projects might find you singing, "Where did my drive go?"

If you are crazy for even more Apple Loops and want to stay with Apple products, you can drop another $199 and buy Apple's Soundtrack appli-cation. It not only gives you Apple Loops not already in your repertoire, but it also gives you a whole other application that allows you to sync to video and other cool tricks. If you don't want to lay down the $199 for Soundtrack, don't fret. If you have the disk space and you still can't get enough, there are even more third-party expansion options.

THIRD-PARTY GARAGEBAND EXPANSION OPTIONS

If you are willing to do a little hunting on the Internet, you will soon find that you can Google up some free Apple Loops. That's right—FREE! What's the catch? Like Apple, some of these bigger companies know once you're hooked, you'll be back for more. And like the old saying goes, "Next time it'll cost you." At press time, there are hundreds of commercial CDs of Apple Loops available. That said, there are also many good, free, no-strings-attached sources for Apple Loops out there.

Here are a few sources for Apple Loops that we found:

- **Drums on Demand**—http://www.drumsondemand.com/
- **BitShift Audio**—http://www.bitshiftaudio.com/
- **SampleNet**—http://www.samplenet.co.uk/
- **Sound Shopper**—http://www.soundshopper.com/

New sites are springing up all the time, so you may also want to search for "GarageBand Apple Loops" on the Web.

GarageBand musicians do not live by Apple Loops alone. In fact, there is a whole world of plug-in Software Instruments and audio effects out there. These plug-ins work for GarageBand and are called *Audio Units*. Audio Units are an Apple standard for third parties to create audio plug-ins that work with OS X audio applications, including GarageBand, Soundtrack, Logic, and many more. Like Apple Loops, there are both free and commercial Audio Units available to expand your GarageBand.

notes

In addition to these sources of Apple Loops, we show you how to roll your own Apple Loops in Chapter 9, "Making Your Own Loops."

We go into depth about how to use Audio Units and where to find them in Chapter 8, "Making Your Own Software and Real Instruments."

CONFIGURING YOUR STUDIO

You can make music using just GarageBand and your Mac; however, if you really want use GarageBand to its full potential, you will need some additional equipment. Fortunately, its the kind of gear that many musicians already possess from doing live gigs or from having set up a home studio in the past.

In this appendix we'll show you how to hook all that stuff up to your Mac so that GarageBand can live up to your expectations and allow you to create that mega-hit that's rolling around in your brain just waiting to get out.

MONITORING

The most important pieces of gear in a studio are a good set of monitoring speakers. Repeat after me: The most important pieces of gear in a studio are a good set of monitoring speakers. Remembering this will save you many heartaches and wasted hours.

If you are monitoring through little popcan "computer" speakers, your magnum opus may sound like mouse excrement in a popcan when played back on a decent system. In addition to a good set of speakers, if you are going to be doing any recording with a microphone, you are going to need a decent set of closed or semi-closed headphones.

Speakers basically come in two varieties: powered speakers with amplifiers built in to their enclosures and passive or nonpowered speakers, which need to be hooked up to an amplifier.

Nowadays, powered speakers have become more popular in computer-based studios. These speakers usually combine the convenience of self-contained units with the good sound of built-in amplifiers that are matched with the speaker's characteristics.

Good examples of this type of monitors in the $300-a-pair range include the M-audio BX5 studio reference monitors (http://m-audio.com/), the KRK RP5 Rokit monitors, and the Edirol MA-20D Digital Micro monitors. If these are too rich for your blood, you might consider these monitors in the $100 range: the Edirol MA-5D, the JBL Creature 2.1 speakers, or the Altec-Lansing AYP3.

If you decide to go with passive speakers, consider that you will also need an amplifier in your purchasing decision. Some reputable brands of speakers and amplifiers include Yamaha, JBL, Mackie Designs, and Alesis.

Regardless of the type or brand of monitoring speakers that you decide to use, the most important factor is that they sound good to your ears and are fairly accurate.

There are basically two ways to hook up your speakers to your computer. One is directly connecting the sound output of the computer or audio interface to the powered speakers or to the amplifier for unpowered speakers, as shown in Figure B.1. Secondly, if you are using a mixer, you will want to route the output of your computer or audio interface to your mixer and then route the monitor output of your mixer to the powered speakers or to the amplifier for unpowered speakers, as shown in Figure B.2.

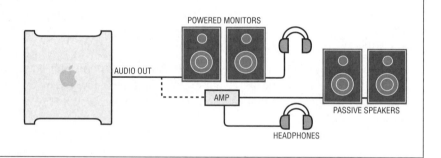

FIGURE B.1
How to hook up monitors without using a mixer. Shown are both powered and nonpowered speaker hook-ups. (Illustration by Annie Kennedy.)

note

Most powered computer speakers automatically mute when you plug in a set of headphones.

The latter method is the better way to go simply because you won't have be constantly unplugging your speakers to plug in headphones, although most amplifiers and some powered speakers have headphone jacks. The important factor here is to have the ability to turn off the speakers while still being able to monitor through the headphones.

In order to avoid feedback when recording to GarageBand with a microphone, you will need to monitor through a set of headphones. Good pairs of professional closed-cup and semi-closed-cup headphones can be found for under $100, so there is no reason to use cheap "walkman"-type headphones. Some good examples of professional headphones are Sony MDR 7505, Sennheiser HD25-sp, Audio-Technica Ath M30, and Fostex t40-RP.

Some people choose to monitor entirely through headphones. While this may seem to be a cheaper alterative to speakers, monitoring through headphones is fatiguing as well as potentially dangerous to your hearing.

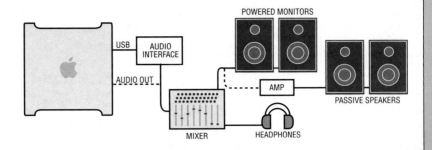

FIGURE B.2
This diagram shows how to hook up both powered and passive monitors using a mixer. Impress your friends with this tricky setup. (Illustration by Annie Kennedy.)

PROTECTING YOUR EARS

If you think about it, hearing is perhaps the most important ability of a musician or just plain lover of music. It is bad enough that everybody's hearing degrades over time, but to accelerate that process is, to say the least, unwise.

Exposing yourself to music (or any noise) over 90Db in loudness over a period of time can cause hearing loss in the form of not being able to hear soft or high-frequency sound, ringing in the ears, and total hearing loss.

If you are a performer, wear ER-15 musician earplugs when on stage. If you are recording or listening to music, try to keep your monitoring levels below 86Db.

If you'd like to read more, there is an excellent article by Clive Williamson at `http://www.symbiosis-music.com/hearing.html`.

'nuff said.

HOOKING UP A MIDI KEYBOARD

You can wile away the hours by playing mixmaster with the thousands of loops within GarageBand, but eventually you'll probably want to play and record your own music. You *can* play GarageBand's excellent Software Instruments using GarageBand's built-in onscreen keyboard, but it isn't the most ergonomic solution for playing music.

If you have bought an electronic music keyboard or synthesizer in the last 10 years, chances are that the thing is MIDI compatible. Without going into what exactly MIDI is, just look on the back of the keyboard for one or two little round connectors with five holes in it. These connectors might even be marked as MIDI in and MIDI out, as shown in Figure B.3. As Martha Stewart would say, "Labeling is a good thing."

You will probably also notice that your Mac doesn't have one of these little five-pin cuties. Your Mac likes its MIDI through one of its USB connectors.

What we need here is some sort of translator. Enter the USB/MIDI interface. A USB/MIDI interface is generally a little box with a USB connector on one side and two or more MIDI connectors on the other side, just like the ones shown in Figure B.4.

> **tip**
>
> Most USB MIDI interfaces only include the interface and a USB cable. Chances are that you will have to purchase MIDI cables separately.

FIGURE B.3
These are typical MIDI connectors. Notice the convenient labeling. (Photo by Jay Shaffer.)

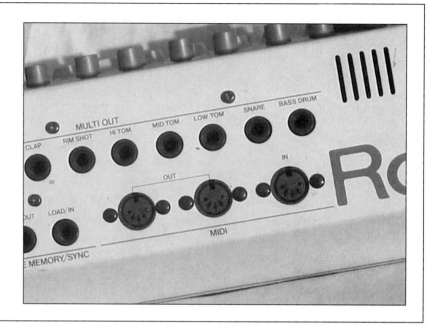

If you are really lucky, your interface will come with some software to install. Just make sure your Mac and the interface are speaking the same language.

FIGURE B.4
This is a USB/MIDI interface featuring dual MIDI inputs and outputs, which means four connectors. (Used with permission: m-audio [www.m-audio.com/].)

If you don't already own a MIDI keyboard and want to purchase one, be aware that there are two kinds of MIDI keyboards out there. There are MIDI keyboards that have their own built-in sound generators and MIDI connectors. These can be used without a computer.

The second kind, called keyboard controllers, don't have any built-in sound generators and usually have a USB interface and must use the computer to make sound. If you are interested in the latter type, Apple has a simple solution for you. Apple teamed up with MIDI giant M-Audio to release a special deal of $99 for the M-Audio Keystation 49e USB MIDI keyboard, as shown in Figure B.5.

This is an excellent keyboard and is available at Apple stores and online at Apple.com. Another type of keyboard to consider is the keyboard controller with a built-in audio interface. These are a bargain in that they provide an all-in-one solution for both audio and MIDI. Some examples of this type are the M-Audio Ozone and the Edirol PCR-A30.

FIGURE B.5
The M-Audio Keystation 49e features 49 keys, USB MIDI, and a 426-cubic inch Hemi. Okay, forget the Hemi part. (Used with permission: m-audio [www.m-audio.com/].)

If you want a musical keyboard that you can unhook from your computer and take to your next karaoke party, you can pick up a consumer-type keyboard with MIDI for about a hundred bucks. With this type, you usually have to buy a USB/MIDI interface.

For the working musician/keyboard player, professional synthesizers and workstations start at about $500 and can go to several thousand dollars. Figure B.6 shows a complete MIDI keyboard setup.

FIGURE B.6
Two possible MIDI hook-ups are shown here: The USB controller hooks directly to the Mac, but the MIDI keyboard has to go through a MIDI interface. (Illustration by Annie Kennedy.)

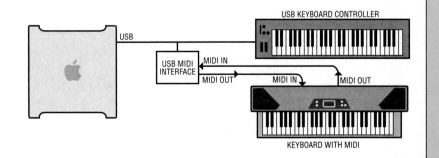

TESTING YOUR MIDI KEYBOARD

Once you have hooked your keyboard to your Mac either via a MIDI interface or via a USB cable and installed any drivers that may have come with your keyboard or interface, it is time to test your MIDI connection. Make sure that your MIDI keyboard is turned on:

1 Launch GarageBand and create a new project by selecting File ···⟩ New.

2 Select GarageBand ···⟩ Preferences. This brings up the Preferences window.

3 Click Audio/MIDI, as shown in Figure B.7.

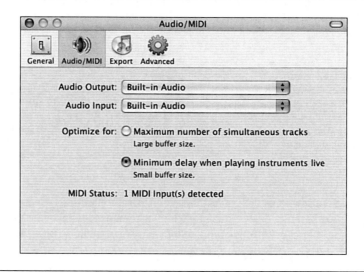

FIGURE B.7
The Audio/MIDI preferences panel shows the MIDI status. One MIDI input detected off the port bow, Captain.

Make sure that the MIDI Status item reads 1 MIDI Input(s) detected. If no MIDI inputs are detected, recheck your hardware connections and make sure that your MIDI keyboard is turned on.

4 Once your MIDI input is detected in the Preferences panel, go ahead and close the panel. Play a note on your keyboard.

Several things should happen. You should hear a piano sound, you should see the green level indicators move as you play a note, and finally you should see a small blue indicator light up in the Track Info window. You should see something like Figure B.8.

FIGURE B.8
MIDI is happenin'!

Input level indicator

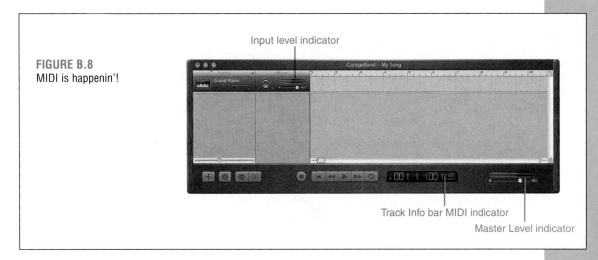

Track Info bar MIDI indicator

Master Level indicator

Now that you have your keyboard working with GarageBand, you will definitely want to check out Chapter 3, "Recording Your Own Music with Software Instruments."

HOOKING UP A GUITAR DIRECTLY TO YOUR MAC

Unlike most music software which seems to be only made for keyboards, GarageBand is made with guitarists in mind.

You don't want to hear about MIDI mumbo jumbo; you just want to plug in your axe and play, man. Hooking your Strat into your PowerBook and laying down a few tracks while riding on the plane between tour dates, that's what it's all about, isn't it?

HOOKING UP TO THE MAC USING AN ADAPTER

Although it does seem a bit unnatural, you can plug your guitar directly into your Mac (if it has an audio in port).

All you need is an adapter. What you need is a mono 1/4'' phono female to stereo 1/8'' mini male adapter.

Once again, Apple comes to the rescue; just go to your local Apple store or go online to Apple.com and get the Monster Instrument Adapter for $19.95. This adapter is also available from Monster Cable directly at `http://monstercable.com/`. The Monster Cable iStudioLink, as shown in Figure B.9, is a simple, elegant solution, well worth the 20 smackers.

Sure, you could probably glom together enough Radio Shack adapters to make this thing work, but you have to ask yourself: Do you really want that monstrosity hanging off of your Mac? And do you want to take a chance at breaking the rather fragile 1/8'' audio input connector on your Mac? That would be a really bad thing.

tip

A guitar's audio signal is weaker than your typical home stereo line-level signal. Although your Mac can handle lower-level signals, you will get a better-sounding signal off your guitar if you use a pre-amp to boost its signal.

FIGURE B.9
The Monster Cable
iStudioLink makes hooking
up your guitar simple.
Simple is good.

Monster Cable iStudioLink™ © 2003 Monster Cable Products, Inc.

HOOKING UP TO YOUR MAC USING A PREAMP

There is another way to hook up your axe directly to your Mac, and that is to use a guitar preamp or DI (direct injection) box. You can get these from several manufacturers for under a hundred bucks. The advantage to using a preamp is that it not only changes your guitar's signal to a true line level signal, but also often has a level control as well as a vacuum tube or tube emulator circuit to add "warmth" to the sound. Figure B.10 shows a typical guitar/mic preamp. These boxes usually have 1/4'' line outs, so you will still need an adapter to connect into your Mac. Figure B.11 shows a couple ways to hook up your guitar.

FIGURE B.10
The ART Tube MP Studio
preamp turns those wimpy
guitar and mic signals into
hefty line level signals.

Photo: courtesy of ART (Applied Research and Technology) www.artproaudio.com

Once you have plugged into your Mac, as shown in Figure B.11, it's time to see if your hot licks are getting into GarageBand.

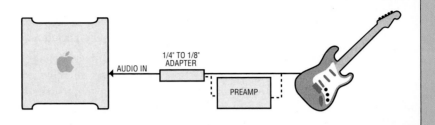

FIGURE B.11
Strat meet Mac. Mac meet Strat. The guitar/Mac love connection. (Illustration by Annie Kennedy.)

TESTING THE CONNECTION

Make sure you have the volume on your guitar turned up; if you are using a preamp, make sure that it is powered on:

1 Launch GarageBand. Create a new project by selecting File ····> New.

2 Select GarageBand ····> Preferences and click Audio/MIDI.

3 Make sure that Built In Audio is selected as the Audio Input. Go ahead and close the preferences panel.

4 Under the Track menu, select New Track.

5 Select Real Instrument and then select Guitars and No Effects. Select the Monitor On radio button, as shown in Figure B.12.

6 Click OK to complete the track creation process.

FIGURE B.12
The New Track window tempts you with the Arena Rock setting, but let's stick to No Effects for now.

Play your guitar. Several things should happen. You should hear your guitar, and you should see the green level indicators move as you play.

Don't worry if it sounds horrible at this point; we just want to make sure that the audio is happening. If you don't hear anything at all and you are seeing the level indicators move, check that Audio Output is set to Built-in Audio in the GarageBand Preferences Audio/MIDI panel and that your speakers are turned on.

If you don't hear anything at all and you are not seeing the level indicators moving, check your connections, make sure that the volume on your guitar is turned up, and that you turned on the preamp if you are using one. If you still don't hear anything, try repeating the new project/new track process. Once you've got everything working, flip back to Chapter 4, "Recording Your Guitar," where we go much more in depth on using your guitar with GarageBand.

HOOKING UP A MICROPHONE DIRECTLY TO YOUR MAC

A guitarist may get his or her flashy solos, but everyone knows the singer is the star of the show. If you want to use GarageBand to show the world your vocal talent, you're going to need to hook up a microphone. Chances are, if you have been singing for a little while, you probably already own a good microphone. If you are just getting started and need to purchase a mic, there are lots of good vocal mics available for under $100. In this section, we'll show you how to connect a professional dynamic microphone to your Mac.

CHOOSING A MICROPHONE

There is one basic difference between a "professional" microphone and a "consumer" mic. Professional mics have a three-pin connector called an XLR connector, as shown in Figure B.13. Consumer mics generally have a 1/4'' or 1/8'' phono-type connector.

FIGURE B.13
This is a typical pro mic with an XLR connector. (Photo by Jay Shaffer.)

The reason that pro mics use XLR connectors is that a three-pin connector allows a less-noisy, balanced connection to other audio gear. Among pro mics, there are two basic types, called dynamic and condenser. *Dynamic* mics are generally the "ice cream cone" type of mic that you see live performers using, as in Figure B.14. *Condenser* mics are usually those big Tylenol capsule-looking mics that you see in recording studios and in Figure B.15.

FIGURE B.14
Audio Technika makes several dynamic microphones for under $100. Perfect for that *Idol* audition. (Photo by Jay Shaffer.)

Dynamic mics are much less fragile than condensers and don't require batteries or power. Dynamics are generally cheaper and are far more common than condensers. By far, the most popular mic on stages around the world is the Shure Sm-58 because it is a very rugged, good-sounding dynamic mic. Sm-58s go for about $150, but many models of similar mics are available for well under $100.

FIGURE B.15
This is a typical condenser microphone shown with a shock mount and stand. Looks dangerous. (Photo by Annie Kennedy.)

Condenser mics are more fragile than dynamic mics, but they are also more sensitive and are better at picking up nuances. They also require power in the form of batteries or via phantom power supplied by a mixer or preamp. Condensers are best used in a controlled environment like a studio and usually start at about $300 and can go up to several thousand dollars.

If you plan on singing live on stage, get a dynamic mic. If you're going to be using the mic in a studio situation and you can afford it, a condenser is a good choice.

In order to be able to plug your microphone into your Mac, you're going to need a couple of adapters. The first adapter is called a *balancing transformer* and converts your microphone cable's three-pin connector to a 1/4'' phono connector. You can find this adapter at your local Radio Shack as catalog # 274-016. The other adapter you need is a mono 1/4'' phono female to stereo 1/8'' mini male adapter, also known as the Monster Cable iStudio Link. You can purchase this adapter at your local Apple store or from Apple.com for $19.95. You can now plug your microphone, via the two adapters, into the Audio In jack on your Mac. While this is a simple solution, it is less than ideal in that we have some rather heavy adapters hanging from a rather fragile jack.

A better, albeit slightly more expensive, solution is to use a microphone preamp such as the one shown in Figure B.10. You can get these from several manufacturers for under a hundred bucks. The advantage to using a preamp is that it not only changes your microphone's signal to a true line level signal, but also often has a level control as well as a vacuum tube or tube emulator circuit to add "warmth" to the sound. These boxes usually have 1/4'' line outs, so you will still need an adapter to connect into your Mac. Figure B.16 shows the connections.

FIGURE B.16
The mic-to-Mac connection is very similar to the guitar-to-Mac connection, but it doesn't require a guitar. (Illustration by Annie Kennedy.)

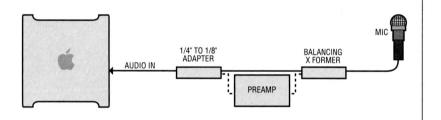

Once you have plugged a mic into your Mac, it's time to see if your hot vocals are getting into GarageBand. If it has a switch, make sure your microphone is turned on; if you are using a preamp, make sure that it also is powered on. Also make sure you are monitoring through headphones and that your speakers are off:

1 Launch GarageBand. Create a new project by selecting File ····> New.

2 Under the GarageBand menu, select Preferences. In the Preferences window click Audio/MIDI.

3 Make sure that Built In Audio is selected as the Audio Input. Go ahead and close the Preferences panel.

4 Under the Track menu, select New Track. In the New Track window, select Real Instrument and then select Vocals and No Effects.

5 Select the Monitor On radio button, as shown in Figure B.17. Finally, click OK to complete the track creation process.

Talk into your microphone. Several things should happen. You should hear your voice, and you should see the green level indicators move as you speak. Don't worry if it sounds horrible at this point; we just want to make sure that the audio is happening. If you don't hear anything at all and you are seeing the level indicators move, check that Audio Output is set to Built-in Audio in the GarageBand Preferences Audio/MIDI panel and that your headphones are connected properly. If you don't hear anything at all and you are not seeing the level indicators moving, check your connections, make sure that your mic is switched on, and that you turned on the preamp if you are using one. If you still don't hear anything, try repeating the new project/new track process. Once you've got the mic connection tested and everything is playing nicely together, flip back to Chapter 5, "Recording Vocals and Other Instruments," where we go much more in depth with using a microphone with GarageBand.

FIGURE B.17
The new vocal track window has all the trick vocal settings.

USING AN AUDIO INTERFACE

The 1/8'' Audio In and Audio Out jacks on your Mac are a simple and convenient way of getting audio in and out of your Mac, but they do have their shortcomings. First off, the 1/8'' stereo jacks are small and fragile and are not considered a good connector for pro-quality audio. Furthermore, the jacks and associated electronics are exposed to possible sources of audio interference inside your computer. Third, while the Mac's built-in 16-bit 44.1KHz (CD-quality) recording was considered sufficient in the past, high-resolution 24-bit recording is the current standard. And some Macs (iBooks in particular) don't even have Audio In jacks.

Enter the audio interface or sound card. Audio interfaces hook up to your Mac either through a USB or FireWire cable. Sound cards are installed in a desktop Macs PCI card slots and often have external "audio breakout" boxes.

note

Different audio interfaces can use USB, FireWire, or a PCI slot to hook into your Mac. PCI interfaces are the fastest and most expensive, whereas USB interfaces are the slowest and least expensive.

For the purposes of this book, we'll lump these together and just call them *audio inter-faces*. These interfaces range from the $39 Griffin iMic all the way up to the "just under" $10,000 Digidesign Pro Tools HD system. Of course, hooking a $10,000 interface is overkill for GarageBand, but it does soften the sticker shock for other interfaces.

What does an audio interface do? It basically takes the analog audio signal from your guitar, microphone, or vintage Mellotron and turns it into a digital signal that your Mac and GarageBand want to see. Nowadays, practically all audio interfaces can do high-resolution 24-bit analog-to-digital conversion. They differ in features like the ability to record more than two simultaneous channels, the types of audio connectors they accept, and built-in preamps and effects. There are even keyboards and mixers with built-in audio interfaces. Figure B.18 shows a standalone interface connection.

Any audio interface is an improvement over your Mac's built-in audio jacks. And a professional-level interface can be had for $200–$300.

> ### tip
> Make sure when buying an interface that it includes Mac OS X driver software and that you install the software according to the manufacturer's instructions.

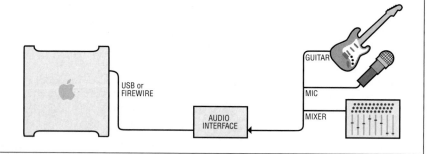

FIGURE B.18
An audio interface connection is like a Fab Five makeover for your Mac's built-in audio jacks. (Illustration by Annie Kennedy.)

To record with GarageBand using an audio interface, you will need to select your interface's driver in the GarageBand preferences window:

1 Launch GarageBand. Create a new project by selecting File ⋯⟩ New.

2 Select GarageBand ⋯⟩ Preferences and click Audio/MIDI.

3 Make sure that your audio interface is selected as the Audio Input.

USING A MIXER

If you visit a professional recording studio, the dominating feature in the control room is the console or mixer; the mixer is the audio nexus of a recording studio. On a much smaller scale, an audio mixer can serve as the nexus for your GarageBand studio.

A four- to eight-channel mixer will allow you to route audio to and from your Mac without the hassle of constantly plugging and unplugging cables from your Mac. It will also serve as a convenient place to hook up and control multiple microphones, guitars, and other instruments. Another important function of a mixer is to allow control of your studio's monitors and headphones.

Small recording mixers are available from such manufacturers as Mackie Designs, Tascam, Edirol, and Samson in the $100–$400 range. Some mixers include a built-in digital audio interface and software controls that add to their value.

THE ULTIMATE GARAGEBAND STUDIO

Although you can start making music with just GarageBand, your Mac, and a set of headphones, to really unleash GarageBand's potential you need some additional hardware.

The ultimate GarageBand studio could end up costing a couple thousand dollars if you purchase all the gear new and separately. Figure B.19 shows a studio configuration with separate components.

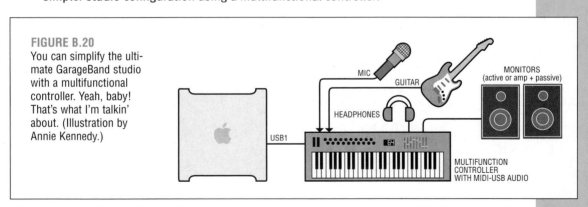

FIGURE B.19
Behold, the ultimate GarageBand studio with separate components. Impressive! (Illustration by Annie Kennedy.)

Fortunately, by using some secondhand gear or buying multifunctional equipment, you can reduce both your investment and studio complexity substantially.

Several manufacturers are now making multifunctional controllers that combine a MIDI keyboard controller with mic and instrument inputs, monitor mixing, and an audio interface into one unit.

We highly recommend this approach. Products of this type include the Edirol PCR-A30, the M-Audio Ozone, and the Novation Remote 25 Audio. Figure B.20 shows a somewhat simpler studio configuration using a multifunctional controller.

FIGURE B.20
You can simplify the ultimate GarageBand studio with a multifunctional controller. Yeah, baby! That's what I'm talkin' about. (Illustration by Annie Kennedy.)

For the same kind of money that you would spend for a day of professional recording studio time, you can create your own GarageBand studio that is functionally pretty darn close to a professional studio. At least it'll do until you get that multimillion dollar recording contract.

KEYBOARD SHORTCUTS

Just like with any software tool, GarageBand allows you to be more efficient by mastering keyboard shortcuts. It is not important that you memorize these lists. But instead, use them to find things that you commonly do, and then learn the shortcuts for those common tasks.

Of course, you can also see many of these shortcuts by choosing the menu items. But others aren't shown anywhere but in the documentation.

MENU SHORTCUTS

These shortcuts allow you to access menu choices without touching your mouse:

Menu Action	Shortcut
GarageBand ⟶ Preferences Dialog	⌘-, (comma)
GarageBand ⟶ Hide GarageBand	⌘-H
GarageBand ⟶ Hide Others	⌘-Option-H
GarageBand ⟶ Quit GarageBand	⌘-Q
File ⟶ New Song	⌘-N
File ⟶ Open Song	⌘-O
File ⟶ Close Song/Window	⌘-W
File ⟶ Save	⌘-S
File ⟶ Save As	⌘-Shift-S
Edit ⟶ Undo	⌘-Z
Edit ⟶ Redo	⌘-Shift-Z
Edit ⟶ Cut	⌘-X
Edit ⟶ Copy	⌘-C
Edit ⟶ Paste	⌘-V

Edit ⟶ Select All	⌘-A
Edit ⟶ Split	⌘-T
Edit ⟶ Join Selected	⌘-J
Track ⟶ Hide Track Mixer	⌘-Y
Track ⟶ Show Track Info	⌘-I
Track ⟶ Show Master Track	⌘-B
Track ⟶ New Track	⌘-Option-N
Track ⟶ Delete Track	⌘-Delete
Control ⟶ Metronome	⌘-U
Control ⟶ Snap to Grid	⌘-G
Control ⟶ Show Loop Browser	⌘-L
Control ⟶ Show/Hide Editor	⌘-E
Window ⟶ Minimize	⌘-M
Window ⟶ Keyboard	⌘-K
Help ⟶ GarageBand Help	⌘-?

GENERAL GARAGEBAND WINDOW SHORTCUTS

These shortcuts aren't as obvious as the previous ones. But they can also be the most useful as they allow you to quickly perform some of the most repeated tasks:

Action	Shortcut
Play/Pause	Spacebar
Go to Beginning	Home or Z
Go to End	End or Option-Z
Previous Measure	Left
Next Measure	Right
Page Back	Page Up
Page Forward	Page Down
Zoom In	Ctrl-Left
Zoom Out	Ctrl-Right
Select Previous Track	Up
Select Next Track	Down
Mute/Unmute Selected Track	M
Solo/Unsolo Selected Track	S
Show/Hide Track Volume Curve	A
Delete Selection	Delete
Record Start/Stop	R
Cycle Region On/Off	C
Raise Master Volume	⌘-Up arrow
Lower Master Volume	⌘-Down arrow

TRACK INFORMATION WINDOW SHORTCUTS

You can use these shortcuts when you select a track and bring up its information window. You can also use them when you create a new track and are presented with the same window in order to set up the new track:

Action	Shortcut
Previous Category or Instrument	Up arrow
Next Category or Instrument	Down arrow
Switch to Category Column	Left arrow
Switch to Instrument Column	Right arrow
Toggle Between Real and Software Instrument	Tab

GARAGEBAND SOFTWARE INSTRUMENTS

G arageBand comes with 65 Software Instruments. It puts them into 12 groups. Here is a list.

BASS

Deep Round Synth Bass
Fingerstyle Electric Bass
Fretless Electric Bass
Muted Electric Bass
Slapped Electric Bass
Sub Synth Bass
Tight Synth Bass
Upright Jazz Bass

DRUM KITS

Dance Kit
Hip Hop Kit
Jazz Kit
Pop Kit
Rock Kit
Techno Kit

GUITARS

Big Electric Lead
Classical Acoustic
Clean Electric
Electric Tremolo
Steel String Acoustic

HORNS

Dub Horns
Live Pop Horns
Pop Horn Section

MALLETS

Aurora Bell
Church Bell
Music Box

ORGANS

Cathedral Organ

Classic Rock Organ

Jazz Organ

Pop Organ

Smooth Dance Organ

PIANOS AND KEYBOARDS

Electric Piano

Grand Piano

Smokey Clav

Smooth Clav

Swirling Electric Piano

Whirly

STRINGS

Lunar Strings

Hollywood Strings

Orchestral Strings

SYNTH BASICS

Circuit Dialog

Constellation

Martian Lounge

Modern Prophecy

Planetarium

Sequence Element 1

Sequence Element 2

Space Harpsicord

Star Sweeper

SYNTH LEADS

Arena Run

Blip Side

Cheerful Trance

Future Flute

Ominous Dancefloor

Riffy Fifths

Synchro Nice

WOODWINDS

Alto Sax

Pop Flute

Tenor Sax

SYNTH PADS

Angelic Organ

Aquatic Sunbeam

Cloud Break

Cosmic Reflection

Falling Star

Mercury Wash

Silicon Strings

EFFECTS LIST

Following is a reference list of all the effects that are included with GarageBand. The effects and what each effect does are covered in Chapter 8, "Making Your Own Software and Real Instruments."

BUILT-IN EFFECTS

The built-in effects are specific to Garage Band and are used to make up many of GarageBand's Real and Software Instruments.

In the list, we note whether the effect is a hard-wired part of the instrument or is selectable.

Also, we list the Apple-provided presets for each effect:

- Compressor (all instruments)
- Equalizer (all instruments):
    - Add Brightness
    - Add Fullness to Snare
    - Add Sharpness
    - Bass Boost
    - Big Drum
    - Brighten Strings
    - Clear Vocals
    - Drum Refresh
    - Flat
    - Hi-Fi
    - Improve Guitars
    - Increase Bass Pluck
    - Mid Reduce
    - Reduce "S"
    - Stronger Bass
    - Vocal Presence

- Reverb (all instruments):
    - Bright Cathedral
    - Cathedral
    - Club
    - Dance Reverb
    - Dark Cathedral
    - Dark Cave
    - Empty Arena
    - Large Cathedral
    - Large Chamber
    - Large Hall
    - Large Stage
    - Living Room
    - Medium Chamber
    - Medium Hall
    - Moon Dome
    - Scape
    - Small Chamber
    - Small Club
    - Small Dome

- Echo (all instruments) :
    - Ambient Delay
    - Dance Echo A
    - Dance Echo B
    - Dark Eight Note Echo
    - Dark Quarter Note Echo
    - Dub Delay A
    - Dub Delay B
    - Electric Shock
    - Endless Loop
    - Half Note Echo
    - Quarter Note Echo
    - Rock N Roll
    - Shift to Bright
    - Sixties Echo Effect

- Gate (Real Instruments only)
- Treble Reduction (selectable):
    - Hard
    - Medium
    - Soft

- Bass Reduction (selectable) :
    - Hi Pass
    - Remove Bass
    - Remove Deep Bass

- Distortion (selectable) :
    - Distortion 1
    - Distortion 2
    - Distortion 3
    - Distortion 4

- Overdrive (selectable) :
    - Drive 1
    - Drive 2
    - Drive 3

- Bitcrusher (selectable) :
    - 6 Bit Resynth
    - Classic 8 Bit
    - Demaged Bits
    - Digitizer
    - Soft Bit Reduction
    - Wave Destruction

- Automatic Filter (selectable) :
    - Deep and Slow Resonance
    - Downbeat Saw
    - Fast Saw Filter
    - FM Filter
    - Resonance Filter
    - Sixtienth Pulse
    - Soft Auto Wah
    - Two Bars Down Filter

- Chorus (selectable) :
  - Faster Modulation
  - Light Chorus
  - Medium Chorus
  - Smooth Chorus
  - Spread Stereo
  - Stage Chorus

- Flanger (selectable) :
  - Full Range
  - Make Wide
  - Medium Flange
  - Organic
  - Resonator
  - Soft Flange
  - String Flange

- Phaser (selectable) :
  - Circle Phases
  - Deep Phase
  - Old Phaser
  - Singing Phase
  - Slow & Deep
  - Surrounding

- Tremolo (selectable) :
  - Circular Structure
  - Fast Pan
  - Leslie Rotor
  - Medium Pan
  - Mono Tremolo
  - Slow and Wide
  - Soft and Fast
  - Ultra Pan

- Auto Wah (selectable) :
  - Bass Snap
  - Bass Wah
  - Crunch Wah
  - Cry Baby
  - Filter Ducks
  - Hi Pass Autofilter
  - Light Peak
  - Static Peak
  - Wow

- Amp Simulation (selectable) :
  - American Clean
  - American Crunch
  - American Overdrive
  - British Crunch
  - British Lead

INCLUDED AUDIO UNIT EFFECTS

Audio Unit effects are Apple's professional-level plug-in effects and can be used by other programs as well as GarageBand. See Chapter 8 for a description of what each effect does:

- AUBandpass
- AUDynamicsProcessor
- AUMultibandCompressor
- AUDelay
- AUGraphicEQ
- AUHighShelfFilter
- AUHipass
- AULowpass
- AULowShelfFilter
- AUMatrixReverb
- AUParametricEQ
- AUPeakLimiter

GENERAL MIDI INSTRUMENTS LIST

In addition to the Software Instruments that come with GarageBand, you can also create your own Software Instruments that access the QuickTime MIDI music instruments, also referred to now as the QuickTime Music Synthesizer. To do this, you need to set the Generator type of the instrument to DLSMusicDevice. Then you can use your musical keyboard or other MIDI device to specify the instrument from the general MIDI list. There are plenty to choose from, so it would be handy to have a reference list.

You can read about how to access these instruments in the section "The Secret of the DSLMusicDevice" in Chapter 8, "Making Your Own Software and Real Instruments."

PIANO

001 Acoustic Grand Piano
002 Bright Acoustic Piano
003 Electric Grand Piano
004 Honky Tonk Piano
005 Electric Piano 1
006 Electric Piano 2
007 Harpsichord
008 Clavinet

CHROMATIC PERCUSSION

009 Celesta
010 Glockenspiel
011 Music Box
012 Vibraphone
013 Marimba
014 Xylophone
015 Tubular bells
016 Dulcimer

ORGAN

017 Drawbar Organ
018 Percussive Organ
019 Rock Organ
020 Church Organ
021 Reed Organ
022 Accordion
023 Harmonica
024 Tango Accordion

GUITAR

025 Nylon Acoustic Guitar
026 Steel Acoustic Guitar
027 Jazz Electric Guitar
028 Clean Electric Guitar
029 Muted Electric Guitar
030 Overdrive Guitar
031 Distorted Guitar
032 Guitar Harmonics

BASS

033 Acoustic Bass
034 Electric Fingered Bass
035 Electric Picked Bass
036 Fretless Bass
037 Slap Bass 1
038 Slap Bass 2
039 Synth Bass 1
040 Synth Bass 2

STRINGS/ORCHESTRA

041 Violin
042 Viola
043 Cello
044 Contrabass
045 Tremolo Strings
046 Pizzicato Strings
047 Orchestral Harp
048 Timpani

ENSEMBLE

049 String Ensemble 1
050 String Ensemble 2 (Slow)
051 Synth Strings 1
052 Synth Strings 2
053 Choir Aahs
054 Voice Oohs
055 Synth Choir
056 Orchestral Hit

BRASS

057 Trumpet
058 Trombone
059 Tuba
060 Muted Trumpet
061 French Horn
062 Brass Section
063 Synth Brass 1
064 Synth Brass 2

REED

065 Soprano Sax
066 Alto Sax
067 Tenor Sax
068 Baritone Sax
069 Oboe
070 English Horn
071 Bassoon
072 Clarinet

PIPE

073 Piccolo
074 Flute
075 Recorder
076 Pan Flute
077 Bottle Blow
078 Shakuhachi
079 Whistle
080 Ocarina

SYNTH LEAD

081 Synth Square Wave
082 Synth Sawtooth Wave
083 Synth Calliope
084 Synth Chiff
085 Synth Charang
086 Synth Voice
087 Synth Fifths Sawtooth Wave
088 Synth Brass & Lead

SYNTH PAD

089 New Age Synth Pad
090 Warm Synth Pad
091 Polysynth Synth Pad
092 Choir Synth Pad
093 Bowed Synth Pad
094 Metal Synth Pad
095 Halo Synth Pad
096 Sweep Synth Pad

SYNTH EFFECTS

097 SFX Rain
098 SFX Soundtrack
099 SFX Crystal
100 SFX Atmosphere
101 SFX Brightness
102 SFX Goblins
103 SFX Echoes
104 SFX Sci-fi

ETHNIC

105 Sitar
106 Banjo
107 Shamisen
108 Koto
109 Kalimba
110 Bag Pipe
111 Fiddle
112 Shanai

PERCUSSIVE

113 Tinkle Bell
114 Agogo
115 Steel Drums
116 Woodblock
117 Taiko Drum
118 Melodic Tom
119 Synth Drum
120 Reverse Cymbal

SOUND EFFECTS

121 Guitar Fret Noise
122 Breath Noise
123 Seashore
124 Bird Tweet
125 Telephone Ring
126 Helicopter
127 Applause
128 Gun Shot

MIDI IMPLEMENTATION CHART

M ost MIDI instruments or other products come with this somewhat arcane chart in the last page of their documentation. It's
called the MIDI Implementation Chart.

The MIDI Implementation Chart is a standardized way to tell which
parts of the MIDI standard are recognized or implemented in a particular MIDI product.

We've heard a clamor on the various GarageBand forums where users
are trying to figure out just which MIDI commands are implemented by
GarageBand. Since Apple didn't include a MIDI Implementation Chart
for GarageBand, we thought we would put one together ourselves as a
service to the advanced GarageBand user community.

MIDI IMPLEMENTATION CHART FOR THE DLSMUSICDEVICE AND GARAGEBAND

This is not an official Apple chart. It was derived entirely through
experimentation.

For Table G.1, *O* means supported, whereas *X* means not
supported:

Table G.1 MIDI Implementation Chart

Function		Recognized DLSMusicDevice	Recognized GarageBand	Remarks
Basic channel	Default	1 - 16	1 - 16	
	Changed	1 - 16	1 - 16	
Mode	Default	Mode 3	Mode 3	
	Messages	X	X	
	Altered	X	X	
Note number		0 - 127	0 - 127	
Velocity	Note on	O	O	
	Note off	X	X	
Aftertouch	Key	X	X	
	Channel	X	X	
Pitch bend		O	O	
Control change	0, 32	O	X	Bank select (MSB, LSB)
	7	O	X	Volume
	10	O	X	Pan position
	71	O	X	Filter Resonance (affects filter Q)
	74	O	X	Filter Brightness (affects cutoff frequency)
	91	O	X	Send to reverb (reverb depth)
	93	O	X	Send to chorus (chorus depth)
	100, 101	O	X	RPN (LSB, MSB) - reserved
	120	O	X	All sound off
	121	O	X	Reset all controllers
	123	O	X	All notes off
Program change		0 - 127	X	
System exclusive		?	X	
System common	Song position	X	X	
	Song select	X	X	
	Tune request	X	X	
System realtime	Clock	X	X	
	Commands	X	X	
Aux. messages	All sounds off	O	X	
	Reset all controllers	O	O	
	Local on/off	X	X	
	All notes off	O	O	
	Active sensing	X	X	
	System reset	X	X	

GENERAL MIDI DRUM KEY MAP

When you use the keyboard to play a musical instrument, each key represents a different note of the same instrument. But drum Software Instruments assign a different instrument to each note.

The map shown in Figure H.1 is the General MIDI drum map guideline; different drum kits may map slightly different instruments to a key. For example, one drum kit might have a handclap mapped D#1 (the standard), but another kit might have a snare roll mapped to D#1. Overall, though, drum kits for the most part conform to this map.

It is handy, therefore, to have a chart showing which keys map to which part of a standard drum kit.

FIGURE H.1
With GarageBand's virtual drum kits, you can forego the drumsticks (and the drummer).

	A3: Open Triangle
G#4: Mute Triangle	G4: Open Cuica
F#4: Mute Cuica	F4: Low Wood Block
	E4: Hi Wood Block
D#4: Claves	D4: Long Guiro
C#4: Short Guiro	C4: Long Whistle
	B3: Short Whistle
A#3: Maracas	A3: Cabasa
G#3: Low Agogoll	G3: High Agogo
F#3: Low Timbale	F3: High Timbale
	E3: Low Conga
D#3: Open Hi Conga	D3: Mute Hi Conga
C#3: Low Bongo	C3: Hi Bongo
	B2: Ride Cymbal 2
A#2: Vibra Slap	A2: Crash Cymbal 2
G#2: Cowbell	G2: Splash Cymbal
F#2: Tambourine	F2: Ride Bell
	E2: Chinese Cymbal
D#2: Ride Cymbal 1	D2: High Tom
C#2: Crash Cymbal 1	C2: Hi Mid Tom
	B1: Low Mid Tom
A#1: Open Hi Hat	A1: Low Tom
G#1: Pedal Hi Hat	G1: High Floor Tom
F#1: Closed Hi Hat	F1: Low Floor Tom
	E1: Electric Snare
D#1: Hand Clap	D1: Acoustic Snare
C#1: Side Stick	C1: Bass Drum
	B0: Acoustic Bass Drum

Not all drum kits conform exactly to the same drum map.

ONLINE RESOURCES

GARAGEBAND AND MAC AUDIO SITES

It seemed that the instant GarageBand was announced, an Internet community sprang up overnight. Here are some sites that have up-to-date news and information about GarageBand and Mac audio in general.

Introducing GarageBand

http://www.apple.com/ilife/garageband/

This is Apple's official product information page.

MacJams

http://www.macjams.com/

This is a large site with GarageBand and Mac audio news, articles, forums, and lots of links.

MacTeens

http://macteens.com/

A site for younger Mac fiends.

MacInTouch

http://www.macintouch.com/garageband.html

This is another large site with all sorts of useful Mac information.

The GarageDoor

http://www.thegaragedoor.com/

Here is a site full of GarageBand tips and tricks.

MacMusic

http://www.macmusic.org/

This site contains news and tons of Mac music software links. You must register (free) to see all this site's content.

Harmony Central

http://www.harmony-central.com/Software/Mac/

This is a site with links to Mac audio-related downloads.

Mac Audio Guy

http://www.macaudioguy.com/

This is Jay Shaffer's own site, and it contains sample files and updates for this book.

OSX Audio

http://www.osxaudio.com/`

Here is a Mac OS X–oriented audio site.

Shareware Music Machine

http://www.hitsquad.com/smm/

This is a huge list of Mac audio shareware.

Audio Units

http://www.audio-units.com/

This is a site with all you ever wanted to know about Audio Units.

SOURCES FOR LOOPS

Apple Loops are popping up faster on the Web than you can download them. Here are a few sites that have Apple Loops as well as some that just have loops that you can convert to Apple Loops:

Drums on Demand

http://www.drumsondemand.com/

This site features a collection of drum loops.

BitShift Audio

http://www.bitshiftaudio.com/

Check out the free set of Apple Loops at http://www.bitshiftaudio.com/products/bbb/free_bee.html.

SampleNet

http://www.samplenet.co.uk/

Here is a huge sample and loop resource.

SoundShopper.com

http://www.soundshopper.com/

This is a list of commercial and free loops.

MAC AND MUSIC MAGAZINES

Here are some offline resources with online counterparts:

MacAddict

http://www.macaddict.com/

This is the ultimate Macintosh magazine, of course.

Future Music

http://www.futuremusic.co.uk/hl_news.asp

This is a UK music and audio magazine.

Computer Music

http://www.computermusic.co.uk

Sister magazine to *Future Music*. This mag often has great software CDs.

Electronic Musician

http://www.emusician.com/

Here is America's best electronic music magazine.

MUSIC SHARING SITES

There are also some places where you can upload and share the music you create:

http://www.icompositions.com/

http://www.macjukebox.net/

http://www.macband.com/

http://www.macidol.com/

GEAR RETAILERS

These sites have the hardware and software goodies to help you make the most of GarageBand:

Apple Store

http://store.apple.com/

Where else? Apple has a selection of gear related to GarageBand, as well as the expansion Jam Pack.

M-Audio

http://m-audio.com/index.php

M-Audio is a Mac MIDI giant. Check out a couple of MIDI devices from M-audio in Appendix B, "Configuring Your Studio."

Audio MIDI

http://www.audiomidi.com/

This is a California-based online retailer.

Musician's Friend

http://www.musiciansfriend.com/

This is the world's largest music gear company.

ART

http://www.artproaudio.com/

ART (Applied Research and Technology) is a manufacturer of preamps and other signal processing gear. You'll find an example of one of its preamps in Appendix B.

Monster Cable

http://www.monstercable.com/

Manufacturer of high-quality cables and interconnects for audio, video, and computers. Refer to Appendix B for more information.

REFERENCES

These sites are valuable references for music and recording:

MIDI Manufacturers Association

http://www.midi.org/

This organization is the keeper of the MIDI standard.

The Rane Pro Audio Reference

http://www.rane.com/digi-dic.html

Here is an audio terminology bible.

INDEX

How can we make this index more useful? Email us at indexes@quepublishing.com

C

auto wah effects, 215

automatic filter effects, 214

bass reduction effects, 214

bitcrusher effects, 214

chorus effects, 215

Compressor, 133, 137, 213

deleting, 92

distortion effects, 214

Echo, 136, 214

Equalizer, 134, 137, 213

flanger effects, 215

Gate, 133, 214

hearing, 133

master track effects, 92-94

overdrive effects, 214

phaser effects, 215

Reverb, 136-137, 214

rock song mixes, 98-99

treble reduction effects, 214

tremolo effects, 215

vocal effects, 74

changing, 75

modifying, 76

Electric Clavinet generator edit window, 129-130

Damper slider, 130

Volume slider, 130

Electric Piano generator edit window, slider controls, 121

Electronic Musician **Web site, 227**

⟨⋯EMBED⋯⟩ tag, 112

embedding songs in Web pages, 111-112

emptying GarageBand window, 12-13

end of song markers, 101-102

Ensemble group list (Audio Unit Instruments), 218

Equalizer edit window, parameters, 134

Equalizer effects, 134, 137, 213

error messages, Unable to continue, 7

Ethnic group list (Audio Unit Instruments), 219

exiting cycle recording, 39-40

expanding

Loop Browser button selection, 14

Onscreen Musical Keyboard, 33

expansions

GarageBand Jam Pack, 189

Soundtrack software, 189

Export to iTunes command, 103

exporting

parts of songs, 101

songs to iTunes, 103-105

extending loops, 19

F

fade-outs in rock songs, building, 69

fading tracks, 21

Fast Forward button (GarageBand control bar), 36

Fav column check box (Loop Browser), 16

favorites, loops

clearing favorite lists, 17

tagging as, 16

viewing, 16

feedback

microphones, 192-193

monitoring (headphones), 72-73, 83

Feedback slider

Flanger effect edit window, 141

Phaser effect edit window, 141

File Type radio buttons (SoundTrack Loop Utility Property tags), 156

files

MIDI files, 18

song files, saving, 11

Filter for More Relevant Results check box (Preferences dialog), 15

filtering loop searches, 15

Fix Timing button (Track Editor), 42-43

Flanger effect edit window, slider controls, 141

flanger effects, 215

How can we make this index more useful? Email us at indexes@quepublishing.com

How can we make this index more useful? Email us at indexes@quepublishing.com

N

Q - R

S

How can we make this index more useful? Email us at indexes@quepublishing.com

How can we make this index more useful? Email us at indexes@quepublishing.com

How can we make this index more useful? Email us at indexes@quepublishing.com

MONSTER®

iStudioLink™

Connect your instruments to the world of digital music.

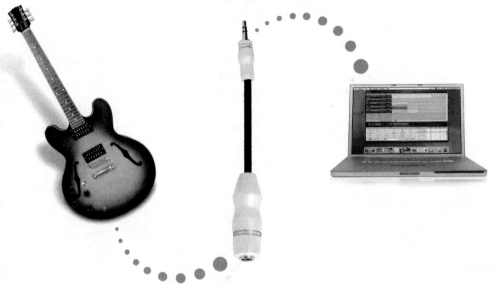

Just Plug in and Play

Start your own portable anytime, anywhere recording studio.

Apple GarageBand™ recording software is really easy to use, and Monster® iStudioLink™ makes it even easier to plug in, play and record right away—without the need for complicated and far more expensive hardware and software. Just plug your mic or instrument cable into the female end of iStudioLink, then plug the male end into your computer's audio line-in/microphone port and you're ready to rock. With iStudioLink and GarageBand, you'll have everything you need to make your next recording sound great, debut it online for download, or burn and share it with iTunes®—maybe even go platinum.

Connect.

Record.

Share.

Mac®

MONSTER®
Get All the Digital Audio Performance You Paid For
Come Visit the Monsters at MonsterCable.com

Perfect for...
 GarageBand™

TUBE VERSATILITY

Announcing the redesigned TPS II™ Tube Preamplifier System and DPS II™ Digital Preamplifier System from ART.

Based on the success of our award-winning TPS and DPS preamp systems, the TPS II™ and DPS II™ feature our improved V3™ Technology (Variable Valve Voicing), which delivers a complete range of newly enhanced presets designed to compliment every microphone, musical instrument and direct signal you process. ART Engineers have improved key feature sets on these units that exceeds that of units costing much more.

Both the TPS II and DPS II also feature variable input impedance, LED input meters, automatic mic/instrument switching, OPL™ (Output Protection Limiting) and more tube warmth than their predecessors. These newly enhanced preamps can accept +20dB peaks while maintaining over 120dB dynamic range and incredibly low distortion. The DPS II includes a versatile insert loop on each channel which provides access for additional signal processing or direct access to our high quality A/D converter. Separate gain controls on analog and digital outputs allow you to optimize the unit for simultaneous applications. Digital outputs include S/PDIF, TOSLINK or ADAT (front panel selectable).

The A/D is front panel adjustable from 44.1 to 96K or syncs to ADAT or external word clock (32KHZ to 100KHZ). You can patch into any ADAT stream and select which pair (or all) of channels the DPS II transmits.

Out of the box, these preamps are ideal for any studio environment or live sound rig. Housed in a single rack space design, for musicians and engineers alike, there is a multitude of uses for the TPS II and DPS II. Use your TPS II or DPS II for any front end signal processing to smooth out your tones and control levels to your outboard devices. Now that's versatile!

Check one out at your local retailer today! For more info on these or any ART product, visit our website at: www.artproaudio.com.

Celebrating Twenty Years of Audio.

△ART
APPLIED RESEARCH AND TECHNOLOGY

215 Tremont St., Rochester, NY 14608 • USA • 585.436.2720 tel • 585.436.3942 fax • info@artproaudio.com • www.artproaudio.com